DAYS IN NORTH INDIA

DAYS IN NORTH INDIA.

NORMAN MACLEOD, D.D.

PROFUSELY ILLUSTRATED

GYAN

Published by

Gyan Publishing House
5, Ansari Road
Daryaganj, New Delhi-110002
Phone: 011-47034999, 9811692060
E-mail: books@gyanbooks.com

Distribution Network
gyanbooks.com
India, USA, Canada, UK, Australia, France

ISBN: 978-81-212-9336-5 (PB)
First Published, 1870

2nd Impression 2023

Printed at: Gyan Press, Delhi.

DAYS IN NORTH INDIA

AUTHOR: NORMAN MACLEOD

DAYS IN NORTH INDIA.

THE GREAT ARCH OF DELHI. *Frontispiece.*

DAYS IN NORTH INDIA.

BY

NORMAN MACLEOD, D.D.,

AUTHOR OF "WEE DAVIE," "EASTWARD," ETC., AND EDITOR OF "GOOD WORDS."

PROFUSELY ILLUSTRATED.

PHILADELPHIA:

J. B. LIPPINCOTT & CO.

1870.

CONTENTS.

ILLUSTRATIONS.

DAYS IN NORTH INDIA.

CHAPTER I.

CALCUTTA TO BENARES.

DAYS—only days! very few they were, yet very memorable. A single fortnight to see Benares, Allahabad, Cawnpore, Lucknow, Agra, and Delhi! Still, I am persuaded, every traveler will agree with me that a vast deal of nonsense is talked about the uselessness of brief visits. Want of time may be painfully felt and acknowledged, and yet, nevertheless, how rapidly the most vivid, correct, and enduring impressions may be made! All have felt this who have even for a few minutes gazed through a telescope on some brilliant constellation, or through the microscope on the marvelous creatures scintillating and roving about in a drop of water. Who that has stood even for one hour by Niagara or Vesuvius; gazed at Mont Blanc from Chamouni, or on Jerusalem from Nebi Samwil; stood on the Acropolis, or on the ramparts of Edinburgh Castle; walked through St. Peter's, the cathedrals of Milan and Cologne, or

York Minster; or even looked on any work of art,—and has not felt the power, the wealth, the gain of a few hours, or even of a few minutes? On the other hand, how little, in comparison, may be seen or acquired by "a voyage round the world," notwithstanding the ground voyaged over and the time occupied in it! For months and months, each day as much like the day before as if the ship was anchored in mid-ocean; few places touched at, and still fewer of these being of interest to any human creature! Panama is probably hurried across in a train pursued by fever; then the Sandwich Islands; Japan; Singapore; the Cape; and home! A single day in Benares or Agra, not to speak of famous historical places in Palestine or Europe, is worth the whole trip! Yet the one traveler can say, "I had but a fortnight;" and the other, "I have gone round the world!" Nor do I see that it would have added any value to this journey even if, as in the olden time, I had taken six months round the Cape to reach Calcutta, and other three months by Dak or Palki, to reach Delhi.

I left Calcutta on the evening of the 11th of February. Many friends accompanied me to the railway station at Howrath, across the Hooghly—for a railway bridge does not yet connect Calcutta with its iron roads. But I believe one is about to be erected. My official work in India had now terminated. There were no other mission-stations connected with our church to be visited by me. Dr.

Watson was to do all this alone. Still, wherever I went, and as far as my time and limited opportunities permitted, I made myself acquainted with missionary operations. I did not, however, feel as heretofore the necessity of devoting myself almost exclusively to this one great object for which our church had sent us to India.

In spite of heat and other drawbacks, I experienced now for the first time since leaving home the feelings of the boy quitting school for a fortnight's holiday. I anticipated with delight any glimpse, however transient, of "Holy" Benares, of Cawnpore, of Lucknow, Agra, and Delhi, names which no longer summon up, as of old, mere associations of Oriental splendor, but remembrances of scenes at once the most revolting and tragic, and of adventures the most heroic and exciting.

There is nothing in Calcutta itself which recalls the mutiny. But the moment one enters the railway terminus at Howrah, he cannot fail to remember a famous scene. Intent only on keeping time according to the rules of the company, a station-master with his force tried to resist General Neill and his "lambs," bent upon pushing on to the rescue of our countrymen. The question was practically and promptly settled by Neill putting the stokers and station-master, the drivers and guards of the train under arrest, until all the troops were seated, and whirled off, few of them ever to return.

Soon after dark I found myself alone, rushing along the line which, for upwards of a thousand miles, leads to Delhi. There is little of any interest to attract the eye or break the *ennui* of the long journey. I do not remember any tunnel the whole way. We passed along the shore of the Ganges, though not always close to it, and across plains, except when, at some points, we skirted a low line of hills rising like a line of beach to this ocean of alluvial soil. There was not much visible of any of the towns we passed. The natives who crowded the station-houses were very like the people we saw everywhere. They pushed along in feverish anxiety to get their seats, being frequently encumbered with their bundles of household gear. Their wives and children clung to them all the while, and jabbered with nervous earnestness.

The first-class carriages are very comfortable. Each seat is capable of accommodating six persons, but they are never crowded, the greatest possible consideration being shown to European travelers. They are much more lofty and roomy than ours, and are protected from the sun by double roofs, projecting shades, and Venetian blinds. The mode of accommodating sleepers is very simple and efficient. The portion which forms the cushioned back of the long seats is lifted up like a shelf, and is made fast by straps to the roofs. Large couches are thus formed, each capable, with a little bending of the knees, of giving stretching room to the travelers at night. At every station abundance of cool drinking water is supplied by a *Bhestie*, and earthen jars are sold for a trifle, in which it may be kept cool in the carriage. The refreshment-rooms are at convenient distances, and are well supplied. At many of them the traveler may remain for the night. As there are English officials everywhere, there are no difficulties in getting along. Most travelers are wise enough, however, to provide some luxuries for the journey; and the private box is often resorted to in preference to the refreshment-room. I never saw any native gentlemen traveling in the same compartment with Europeans. This circumstance, however, arises not so much from any repugnance of race, as from customs and habits which make the native repugnant to the European, and the European equally repugnant to the native.

We reached Bankimpore, the station nearest to Patna, next day, and were most hospitably received and entertained by Mr. Richardson the magistrate. Dr. Watson had traveled by Palki to Gyah, some sixty miles off, and returned with our two missionaries, Mr. Clark and Mr. Macfarlane, old friends of mine, that we might confer together at Patna. I was unable to see anything of this great Mahommedan city, but I had the happiness of meeting at the house of Mr. Richardson a large party of our countrymen.

We left Patna next evening, and reached Benares

about midnight. Here we were welcomed by the Rev. Mr. Kennedy, the respected missionary of the London Society, who has long labored in this city. Mr. Clark had returned to Gyah, but Mr. Macfarlane accompanied us as far as Lucknow. Mr. Kennedy had made every preparation to enable us to see as much as possible of the city. The handsome English carriage of the Rajah Sir Deo Naryen Singh was waiting for us at the station, and next day was kindly put at our disposal, and our first visit was to the Rajah.

I may here state that Benares is the finest city in *Doab*, higher or lower. It is on the frontier of the great governmental division called the Northwest Provinces, which to the north, near Umballa, is bounded by the Punjaub, and along its western frontier, south of Oude, by the Himalaya. These magnificent provinces are in area nearly equal to Great Britain, with an average of 361 persons to the square mile. There is a lieutenant-governor, and the provinces are divided into thirty-five districts, with six commissionerships.

But to return to Sir Deo. He was most faithful to the British government during the mutiny, and did us the greatest service. To testify his sincerity he lived with the Resident, and put himself wholly in his power, when things were at the worst. No wonder that he should have had knighthood conferred upon him and the order of the Star of India.

Sir Deo's house and its arrangements seemed in some of their features characteristic of India. The outer gate led into a bare open compound, surrounded by the houses of the servants and dependents. This again led into a beautiful, well-watered garden, with walks of marble, beyond which was a handsome house approached by a double flight of steps, leading to the entrance-door from an elevated terrace. This door was a very narrow one, with a narrow and steep flight of steps conducting to the public rooms above—a species of access which always suggests the idea of defense against sudden attack.

Sir Deo met us at the top of this steep stair, received us very courteously, and conducted us to his drawing-room, which was furnished in the same profuse manner as those we had seen in Calcutta, with European works of art. It is used as a reception-room for European visitors only. Mr. Kennedy acted as interpreter. Sir Deo seemed to be an unaffected man, of much intelligence and common sense. The conversation was on several topics, but it was not of a kind to be reported. He presented us with flowers and scented our handkerchiefs—events of no serious importance. His attendants, like those I had seen in Calcutta, appeared to have a spirit of deep reverence for their master, with the same open-eyed interest in all that we said. Their bearing was much like what I have observed in Highland servants of the olden time—servants, yet friends, in whom a sense of dependence was combined with the social sympathies of what I may call Patriarchal republicanism.

Sir Deo sent a servant to accompany us in our ramble through the city. This servant carried a most imposing "silver stick," which gave one a pleasing sense of his own importance. The means of conveyance put at our disposal to thread the streets of "Holy Benares" were the Rajah's carriage, elephant, and *tonjons*, a sort of open sedan-chair, which is carried by poles resting on the shoulders of the bearers.

After parting with the carriage, where the narrow streets made it impossible for us to proceed in it, we found the elephant waiting for us. I felt awed in the presence of the noble beast! My acquaintance with his kind had been limited to Wombwell's Menagerie and the Zoological Gardens. We had seen only two or three in India, and these did not impress us. It had never been proposed to us to ride upon any, either as a matter of amusement or of business. But here was a proper animal for our use. He was of great size, and of great age. He stood with gouty-like legs, moving his huge ears. He was clothed in a coarse, home-made drapery of skin, fitting loosely to his body, and forming trowsers—not exactly like those exquisite models pictured at railway stations, price 16*s*. A lad sat on his huge head, a thick iron spike in his hand, by which he seemed to touch the creature's thoughts as if by some electric process.

A ladder placed against his side led up to the seat on his summit. It was not possible to look at that small eye of his without questioning one's safety: it was so inquisitive and sagacious, so thoughtful and calculating, that no astonishment would have been felt had he, out of sheer fun, played us any trick, and then shaken his frame with elephantine laughter. Before we ascended he bent his tough gray knees, not, however, until cushions had been laid for them. Then he quietly knelt down. We got up to our seats, feeling very much as if we were on the ridge of a one-storied house. We there held on as if for life, while the mountain heaved, for as he rose on his hind legs he sent us forward, and on his fore legs sent us backward.

At last we got under way. Judging from my own feelings, I was astonished that the people did not laugh, and the windows open that the idle women, albeit in the East, should see the sight. But all seemed to be a matter of course, much as if at home we had hired a cab. On we went, with slow, silent, soft, stately swing. The great ears were below us, and below them the stout tusks, as if to clear the way. Having fully realized our dignity, and being fully convinced that all asses, horses, carriages—even railways—were poor and undignified things when compared with an elephant, and almost wishing that we could have one provided for us as we went to report ourselves to the first general assembly in Edinburgh, we nevertheless quietly hinted that a more humble mode of conveyance would be quite as comfortable; so we descended, with gratitude for our safety.

Apart from our own wishes, the streets made this change necessary. I question if our august friend could have squeezed himself through some of the narrow lanes of Benares. In its structure internally as a city, as well as in other respects which I shall presently allude to, Benares stands alone. The houses are all built of solid stone, obtained from the quarries of Chumar in the immediate neighborhood. They are flanked by houses six or even seven stories high. Whether to gain shade from the burning sun, or as a means of defense against foes, these streets are so narrow as to resemble the *closes* in the old town of Edinburgh. Indeed, if our readers can suppose the closes worming through the whole city with sharp turnings and endless windings, they will have a pretty good idea of the place. There are shops of every kind and for every trade, according to the quarter of the city. All these are open to the street. There are workers in brass and iron, in silver, gold, and jewels; workers of slippers and saddlery; of arms and accouterments; of cloths and Oriental fabrics; of sweetmeats *ad nauseam;* and sellers of grain of every kind. The lower stories in all the houses are the worst, and we sometimes saw cattle stalled in them, and gazing out into the street to add to the peculiarity of the scene.

To a traveler, one of the most remarkable features of Benares is the presence of monkeys. The honor conferred on this animal is not owing to any anticipation of the discoveries of Darwin which have made the genus interesting, as being the possible ancestors of Milton, Shakspeare, and Goethe; but because of certain benefits conferred by the king of the monkeys upon the deities of Hindoo worship, which need not here be inquired into. These funny creatures are fed by pilgrims; they enjoy the happiest, most guileless existence in Benares; and although panics have been occasioned by accidents befalling them—a broken leg having in one instance sent a foreboding gloom over the more religious inhabitants of the city—they themselves seem strangely unconscious of responsibility, and leap, and climb, and jabber, and amuse themselves in a way which is really delightful to their human descendants.

The only shop or factory we had time to visit was that of the famous Brocade of Benares. We threaded our way through many narrow passages, and ascended many narrow stairs, and passed through room after room, until we got into the treasure-room of the gorgeous manufacture. All this difficulty of entrance told of past times, when property was so insecure as to demand means of concealment and defense. When at last we reached the small chamber where the goods were displayed, we fully enjoyed the brilliant spectacle. To see those magnificent gold brocades, costing twenty pounds or even more the yard! Wealth might purchase them, but no wealth, save the wealth of long trained art, could command the exquisite taste they display. Web after web was unfolded, and it was a great enjoyment to gaze on them. Oriental splendor appeared so natural and so refined, that broadcloth and white neck-ties seemed impossible for any one who could clothe himself in such gorgeous costume. To adopt our vulgar, prosaic, commonplace Western suits was like preferring mist and rain to the splendors of sunset. From defective arrangements as to the pay of the clergy, it was impossible for me to patronize this magnificent manufactory. But I gave it all I had to bestow—my enthusiastic admiration.

Our next "Peep" at Benares was from the river. But before taking this peep I must put the reader more *en rapport* with this famous city.

Benares is to the Hindoos what Mecca is to the Mohammedans, and what Jerusalem was to the Jews of old. It is the "holy" city of Hindostan. I have never seen anything approaching to it as a visible embodiment of religion; nor does anything like it exist on earth. Its antiquity is great—how great I do not know. As in the case of most ancient cities, there are in it few remains of the old portions. Perhaps not a single building or even the remains of one exists which dates beyond three or four hundred years, and this owing to the domination of the Moslem, with his hatred of idolatry and idol temples. Even poor, desolate Jerusalem has many more vestiges of the past than Benares. But nevertheless it is now, as it has been for long ages, the grand center of Hindoo worship and veneration. It contains a thousand temples, and tens of thousands of images of all the gods worshiped in Hindostan. To make a pilgrimage to Benares, to visit its shrines, and walk for fifty miles around its sacred territory, even though tottering with age or sickness, and almost crawling on the earth, has for centuries been the highest ambition of the devotee, from Cape Comorin to the Himalayas. And to die in Benares has been the sure passport of millions wishing for glory. The orthodox rulers of territories, small or great, recognized its sanctity; and in person, or by the substitution of their vakeel, have paid their respects and money to it, and sought its blessings. Many nobles have built their palaces in it, and have reared temples, or long flights of stairs, or ghauts, for the convenience of the faithful. Not a few have spent and many still spend the evening of their days within its walls, atoning for their sins by their asceticism, or by their liberal hospitality and largesse to the ever-recipient Brahmins. Benares has been the Vatican, the Oxford and Cambridge, of Hindostan. Here the most learned men of India have lived, studying the Vedas, which to all but the priesthood were sealed books, until they were mastered and published by Max Müller and his learned brotherhood. The pundits of Benares have written learned treatises on grammar, metaphysics, and theology; students from every part of the country come to live with them and study under them. Here, miserable devotees covered with ashes have endured fiercest torments; and holy beggars in crowds have collected their alms. Holy bulls have wandered through the streets, and as gods were revered, being made welcome to eat at every grain shop they were pleased to honor with their attentions. No "melas," or holy fairs, were so attended as those of Benares. Hundreds of thousands every year gathered to this the scene of their solemnities.

Changes to some extent have taken place. The "melas" are not now so well attended. Without much opposition, the bulls have, for sanitary reasons, been denied the freedom of the streets. But the monkeys are as holy and as numerous as ever. As the last convulsive effort of dying Brahminism, the temples increase rather than diminish; and the city is as much as ever "wholly given to idolatry."

The difference between the finest temples in Benares and those in South India is very visible. The former are paltry and contemptible in comparison with the latter. This, I understand, has been occasioned by the Mohammedan persecutions in former days, when the Great Mogul was all and all. Large temples would then have been destroyed, and large shrines were consequently preferred, as being more easily built again if destroyed. The Hindoos never had such freedom under "native" Mohammedan rule as they have enjoyed under the foreign Christian government of Britain.

To visit the temples of Benares would be the labor of weeks, and the profit more than questionable. We visited the chief one, however, the temple of Bisheswar, the idol king of Benares.

The one which we visited was a sort of cathedral. It had nothing imposing in its structure. The lingam predominated, and, in fact, was all in all.

The usual ceremony of worshipers in this temple consists in presenting some flowers to the ugly-looking monster called God. They prostrated themselves before him, and struck the bell, which is in every temple, and then departed. The temples are always wet with the holy water of the Ganges, which is poured on the god, and over every offering. Many of the worshipers throw themselves down before the savage-looking image, and not a few seemed excited by bang. There is a famous well beside the temple, into which flowers were cast, and from whose fetid waters worshipers drank. The people looked utterly stupid and prosaic; many of them were sensual and depraved in appearance, and the whole scene disgusting in the extreme. This impression was not lessened by the sight of figures of bulls carved in stone, reminding one, as they did, of the olden time of Apis and the golden calves, with the condemnation of the Almighty upon them.

We rowed down the river through the city, for two or three miles, in a covered boat. Certainly I

never saw such a striking spectacle in my life. It remains unapproached and unapproachable in my memory. No description can give any adequate idea of the scene. I must refer to the illustration, although even it can only convey an imperfect notion to the reader. The architecture was remarkable; yet no building, unless perhaps the two remarkable minarets, made any distinct impression of beauty or of grandeur upon the mind. Still, as a whole, and with many remarkable *bits*, it was extraordinary. The city rose high from the edge of the grand old river with a strength and imposing majesty (from its height and the vast mass of stone) such as I had not

BOATS ON THE GANGES.

Page 27.

before seen in the East. The river itself flowing in broad and rapid stream formed a splendid foreground

to the picture. Its surface was covered with every kind of out-of-the-way picturesque boat, whose sails,

whether white or saffron-colored, whole or tattered, each made a study. The marvelous line of architecture was of every possible variety of form, the ghauts, or landing-places, having long flights of stairs, and being continued on and on along the river, in such numbers as one never saw before. These stairs were not uniform, but were longer or shorter, broader or narrower, according to each builder's fancy. All,

however, were built of solid stone, massive and apparently enduring. Above these, and mingling with them in utter confusion, were a countless number of temples, small and great. And then, lastly, overtopping these, were fortress-looking stone palaces of rajahs, who had here their town residences, although probably they generally resided in distant parts of India. When one was cool enough—for the spectacle was most exciting—to look at architectural details, how picturesque they were! As to the excellence

THE GHAUT

S, BENARES. Page 31.

of these works as artistic productions I could form no judgment as I floated past—I felt, but could not criticise. And certainly nothing could be more unique than such a first glimpse beneath the bright sun, and the blue sky, of an outline so broken, and of forms so fantastic;—of brightest lights and shadows numberless;—of balconies, verandas, towers, cupolas, oriel windows, projections, recesses, and covered galleries, endless and indescribable! And then there was the absence of every trace of Westernism, for so far as the eye could see, no Englishman had ever visited Benares. There Hindooism had reigned long ere the Romans had landed in Great Britain, and did not seem to have been disturbed.

The ghauts are wholly given to idolatry, and were alive with devotees. Hundreds, nay, thousands, crowded them; many performing their ablutions in the holy waters of the Ganges, and saying their prayers. Thousands, again, grouped round the holy Brahmins, who sit under their white umbrellas, planted like beds of great mushrooms along the river; for, under these, all ceremonies are properly arranged, blessings bestowed, and fees paid. Here the weak, the aged, and the sick who have arrived from long pilgrimages of hundreds of miles, receive spiritual strength and comfort from these sacred waters, or die and enter heaven direct from its gate. On one ghaut smoke constantly ascends from the burning bodies of the dead, and on another the most heinous crimes are being atoned for. Rest is promised to the sinful and weary as the reward of sacrifices, pains, penances, and pay. And all this has been going on for centuries! What knows this spiritual world of Benares about us—and what care we for it! Alas, we are only excited or amused by this antique drama—so strange, so un-European, so old-world is it. Were we ourselves right toward God and man, and had we love to our Father and our brother, we should look at such a spectacle with a very different eye, and experience a poignant sorrow for such ignorance, degradation, and "lying vanities." One spectacle only is more sad and alarming, the idolatries, the mammon worship, the indifference and the formality, the materialism and unbelief which exist at home. Within the heart of the Church of Christ, more than anywhere else, the battles are to be fought and the victories gained, which will insure the spiritual conquest of India, and ultimately convert such a city as Benares into a home of Christian worship.

I have before me a lecture, delivered in December, 1866, by a native, Lingam Lakshmaji Pantlu Garu, before the Benares Institute, which gives anything but a flattering account of "the social status of the Hindoos." Whether his is a correct account or not, I cannot tell. But it is interesting as being the judgment of "one of their own children," who, one would think, must be well informed on the subject. If his statements were untrue, he would hardly dare to give them forth in the city of Benares, and among his own people.

There are about ten missionaries in Benares, supported by the Church Missionary and London Missionary Societies, with schools, native pastors and teachers, and native congregations. Mr. Kennedy, our host, who is connected with the London Mission, and Mrs. Leupoldt of the Church Mission, have labored here for twenty-six years. Here, as in other parts of India, we have evidences that the combined forces of Western culture and civilization, together with education and Christian teaching, are slowly but surely creating a better public opinion, and, if not making many individual converts as yet, are most certainly and surely preparing the way for greater results in the future.

There is also in Benares a very handsome government college, which I had time only to glance at. It seemed full of young men, and was presided over by a distinguished Oriental scholar.

And now, before starting for Cawnpore and Lucknow, I must say a few words about the great mutiny, thoughts of which possess the mind in visiting those cities, just as do thoughts of battle, and thoughts of the bravery of our countrymen, when we visit the field of Waterloo and the ruins of Houguemont.

As we peruse the many narrations of such a terrible time as that of the Indian mutiny, or when in silence and with a full heart we pace over the spots associated with the awful and stirring events which these describe, we find it difficult to "set them in order" before the mind, and to form a clear and precise idea of them, any more than when reading the account of a fleet bravely combating the winds and waves of a furious hurricane, we can follow the evolutions of each vessel, and realize the details of the scene. In the history of the mutiny all seems inextricable confusion. Innumerable pictures rapidly pass before the eye and excite our wonder and our profoundest sympathy: large armies rising against defenseless men, women, and children; officers rudely massacred; inconceivable treachery; robberies; cantonments on fire; miscreants let out of prison; telegraphs destroyed; communication cut off; defenses extemporized; agonized women and children flying by night anywhere to escape the shouts and yells of murderers in pursuit; broken-hearted husbands and fathers, in nakedness and want, wandering through the jungles to seek shelter in vain, and dropping down one by one under disease, or fatigue, or the stealthy hand of the assassin; heroic defenses rising everywhere against fearful odds; with sufferings, agonies, escapes, battles, victories, each and all of tragic interest; culminating at length in the defense and relief of Lucknow, the capture of Delhi, which crown a history of such indomitable courage as cannot be surpassed by that of Greek or Roman fame.

It is strange to be reminded—as one often is—how a new generation has already grown up, who do not remember these occurrences, and know little of them—although to many of us they seem fresh as "the latest intelligence" of the daily newspaper. But the memories of such times must not be allowed to perish! What our nation has suffered and achieved in the past is a precious inheritance to all generations; and her sins and chastisements, as well as her deeds of righteousness and her triumphs, should live in our thoughts as lessons for our warning or for our encouragement.

Those who wish to obtain full and accurate information, gathered from the most authentic sources, regarding the history of the mutiny, will find it in Mr. Kaye's deeply interesting "Sepoy War."* Yet, as the subject of the mutiny was naturally a constant topic of conversation with those whom we met in India who had taken a prominent part in the leading events of that memorable time, I may be permitted to say a few words on the subject.

1. It was not a rebellion of the country against the British rule, but a mutiny of the soldiery—a "Sepoy War" only. Accordingly, as a rule, the natives of power or political influence did not rise against us; while all to whom we had shown kindness, and by whom we had dealt justly, stood bravely

---

* The first volume only has been published as yet.

by us. Men of wealth everywhere, who had anything to lose, did the same. The titular King of Delhi, the deposed King of Oude, Holkar, the miscreant Nana Sahib, and such like, had suffered real or supposed injuries at the hands of our government; while others, from fear or from hopes of booty, were carried away, or forced into the movement by the fierce, and, for a time, apparently successful, Sepoys. But, with such exceptions as these, our enemies were composed of the soldiery—the contents of broken-up jails and gangs of hereditary robbers, who had been kept under control by the sheer power of the government. To these may be added the many to be found everywhere who hoped to get something for themselves in the scramble.

I do not allege, by any means, that the natives did not rebel, owing to their affection or disaffection toward our people and our government.* It must be

* In July, 1867, a confidential circular was issued by the Viceroy to the leading civil administrators in British India, demanding their opinion with reference to the correctness of a doubt expressed by the present Marquis of Salisbury (then Lord Cranbourne), in the House of Commons, as to whether the system of British administration in India possessed, in the minds of the natives, any superiority over the method of government pursued in the Independent States. This called forth about thirty replies, which were published by the Indian government at Calcutta, in December, 1867. In this correspondence the question started is fully treated, and the amplest justice is done to all sides by the men most competent to deal with such a matter. It impresses one very deeply, I think, with the political wisdom, the intellectual grasp, and thorough fairness and honesty, of the leading civilians who practically govern India—and it is full also of deeply-interesting information.

confessed that the English generally are not popular. They are apt to be distant in their manners; to show a large amount of *hauteur* and pomposity; to look at things too much through English spectacles; to be somewhat wanting in social sympathies with foreigners, as well as in the fancy and imagination required to understand Oriental character. And to all this must be added their merely temporary residence in the country, and the utter impossibility of their coming into close contact with the people, owing to wide differences in language, race, and, above all, in the customs and feelings springing out of religion. Thus it is that the Westerns never can be popular with the Easterns, let them govern ever so wisely and well. But whether popular or unpopular, whether, on the whole, wise or unwise, it remains beyond all question that ours is the best government which has ever existed in India. There never was one which has so benefited the *masses* of the country, or given such security to life and property. Nor have any before tried so honestly to do their duty, or been so truly a "terror to evil-doers and a praise to them that do well."

But if there was no enthusiasm for us as a people on the part of any class, there was a positive and undying hatred toward us on the part of the Mohammedans, as well as a growing dislike entertained toward us by the orthodox Hindoos and Brahmins. They easily perceived that their old civilization was being every day, and in many forms, brought into direct antagonism with ours; and were forced to the conclusion that theirs must, in the long run, give way. As to the rural population whom we have most benefited, they often behaved very well and kindly to our people when seeking shelter during the mutiny.* But what could be expected from these rude and ignorant natives, whose own superiors and friends had risen against us? What knew they of past governments, so as to be able to contrast them with our own? All they knew was, that Might alone had a right to claim their homage and respect, and as this seemed no longer to belong to the Feringees, their claims were gone! The peasants and the princes, the ryots and the rajahs, were in some respects alike. All were equally indifferent to the English race; all regarded them as strangers and

---

* Mr. Kennedy, our host while at Benares, published a brief but well-written account of the "Great Mutiny" in October, 1857. In writing on this point he speaks thus:

"To see European gentlemen and ladies fleeing on foot for their lives, in a country about which they had hitherto ridden in carriages as the rulers of the land, was an extraordinary spectacle which drew forth wonder and pity. We have heard of villagers lifting up their hands and giving expression to their astonishment in the strongest terms. Not a few, utterly destitute, wandered among them, and were helped and relieved. We have known of a major's lady, with three children, the youngest thirteen months old, and the eldest not five years, without a rupee, without a change of clothing, without an attendant, wandering about for a fortnight in a very turbulent district, and everywhere treated with pity and kindness, till at last she succeeded in reaching a European station. For every such instance of kindness we fear ten instances of treachery and cruelty might be adduced."

aliens; and all worshiped Power *de facto*, without respect to *de jure*. The difference between them was this, that the poor man thought he might gain something and lose nothing by a revolution, while the rich man believed the reverse; the one supposed that power belonged to the Sepoy, and therefore they followed him; the other believed that it belonged to the government, and therefore they supported it. It was thus not a rebellion, but a mutiny, in which, from various motives, many natives sympathized, but few of any influence assisted either by men or money.

2. But what occasioned this mutiny among our Sepoys, who had so long fought and conquered for us, been trusted by us, and officered by us? This has been all accounted for by the condition of the Bengal army. Its discipline had become lax; its feelings, its whims and prejudices, had been in some respects too much yielded to, while in others they were not sufficiently considered and respected. Above all, the native soldiery apparently held all power in its own hands, and seemed to be able to seize the whole country, and bring back the reign of the Moguls. Moreover, the Crimean and Persian war had prevented British troops from being regularly sent to India. Never had the country, with its treasuries, magazines, and forts, been so entirely given up to native regiments for protection. At Cawnpore, which used to have a strong European garrison, with in-

fantry, dragoons, and artillery, there was but one company of European artillery, and a large native force. In the whole Province of Benares, with a population nearly three times greater than that of all Scotland, when the mutiny broke out, there was only a European force of twenty-five artillerymen and sixty invalid soldiers, while there were everywhere native regiments of infantry, cavalry, and artillery! Nor did the soldiers of the Bengal army, like those of the Madras one, have their wives and families within their lines, their homes being in the North, generally in Oude, so that the mutineers, going north, fled not from their families, but to them. One check against the license and excess that ensued was thus absent. Another feature of the army was the presence in it of so many Brahmins,* who, as I have before remarked,

* Mr. Kennedy, in his account, writes that in the 37th Native Infantry which mutinied in Benares, there were, according to the account of one officer, 400, and to another, 600 Brahmins. He gives the following description of these Brahmins:

"It is commonly thought in Europe that Brahmins are holy men, devoted entirely to religious services; at one time engaged in conducting the worship of the people, and then studying with eagerness the Shastres, which they deem the productions of the gods and sages; now unfolding to the people the meaning of these Shastres, and then, as their spiritual guides, applying their lessons to the varied phases of life; at one time dwelling among the people as their religious teachers, then retiring to the wilderness to give themselves uninterruptedly to devotion and ascetic practices; above all, regarding life with the utmost sacredness, shrinking from taking the life of an ant, far more the life of a human being. To such persons the announcement must be startling, that Brahmins abound in the Bengal army. Residents in India know well that Brahmins form had of late become afraid of both their religion and of their influence being weakened. These fears had been intensified by reports of an intention on the part of government to send them for service abroad, which would destroy their caste; and no doubt the question of the greased cartridges, though chiefly the mere pretext, was also to some extent one of the causes of the mutiny.

---

in many districts a large part of the community; that they are a race, rather than a select class set apart for select work, and that they are obliged, whatever their theoretic views, to engage largely in secular employments for their support. Setting aside the many who find subsistence as priests, performers of ceremonies, religious teachers, plodding scholars, carriers of sacred water, guardians of sacred places, ascetics, and religious beggars, there remains a very large part of the community to be otherwise occupied and supported. A vast number of them are so illiterate that they cannot read a word, but whatever their work may be, they never forget that they are Brahmins. They have had it instilled into their minds from their earliest years, that they are essentially different from and superior to others, and that it is only an iron age that is the cause of their depression. Of their deep humiliation during a large part of the Mussulman rule they know little, and think less; but the most illiterate among them are familiar with the traditions, which represent them as superior even to the gods. In thought they live in the times of which their poets sing, when the world existed only for the glory of the Brahmins. That these men should be proud, and look down on others with contempt, is an inevitable consequence.

"Brahmins, even when illiterate, have first-rate talents for plotting, and with no check from a foreign element in the ranks, it would be strange if their talents were not drawn into exercise. They are also intensely superstitious. They are not high-principled, or even, as a body, orderly in their lives, but their immorality is quite consistent with superstitious zeal. They are superstitious from policy, as well as from education and habit, being well aware that the downfall of Hindooism would be the downfall of that fancied greatness, to which they attach so high a value."

Finally, the annexation of Oude, with expectations of the same policy being followed out in other districts, added fuel to the flame. The people of Oude had no doubt complained to the British resident times and ways without number against the cruelties and tyrannies of their native rulers, and of the lawless oppression which everywhere prevailed. A more worthless and depraved king and court, a more infamous horde of men and women, than that which crowded the palaces of Lucknow never existed upon earth. They lived in the wildest and lowest debauchery, from the half-idiotic king and his ministers down to the troops of fiddlers, dancing-girls, and mountebanks. The country was sick of them. Yet the dethroning of the whole royal race, the annexing of a whole kingdom with its revenues to the British crown, was an extreme, and, to say the least, a doubtful measure, according to the judgment of some of the ablest men in India. And to this was added the unwise treatment of the Thalookdars. These native aristocrats lived in their own feudal castles in the midst of the jungles, defended by their own guns and followers. They might have been gained to our side, but from some of our "hard and fast" red-tapeism they were turned against us, so that the kingdom of Oude was really in rebellion. The soldiers of the Bengal army were deeply affected by this; for they were chiefly recruited from Oude, and all their relatives were there.

But I will not dwell longer upon this subject at present. Other sides and features of the mutiny will fall to be considered as we proceed in our narrative. We must move on to Allahabad, Cawnpore, and Lucknow.

CHAPTER II.

FROM ALLAHABAD TO LUCKNOW.

To a European, the most attractive feature of Allahabad is the Fort. Its huge red sandstone walls and bastions rise with imposing effect from the angle

FORT AT ALLAHABAD.

of ground which, washed by the Jumna and Ganges, forms the terminating point of the district named the

Doab. This fort, it is said, was originally Hindoo. It may be so; but, beyond doubt, with the exception of the last scientific touches given to it by the British, the great Akbar made it what it now is. He it was who reared its magnificent gateway, and great hall of audience within, both of which bear witness to the stateliness of his designs.

The two most interesting sights within the fort are an underground temple, of vast antiquity, which we visited, and a *lat* or pillar of Asokas, erected three centuries before Christ, recording certain statutes in an old character of the ancient Pali language.

But I confess that, during my brief visit to the North, my thoughts were wholly occupied by the events of the great mutiny of 1857, at least until I reached Agra and Delhi, whose magnificent architectural remains in some degree broke the mesmeric influence of that stirring time. Many persons may very naturally suppose that these events are so fresh in the memory of our nation as to render any notice of them unnecessary; but we forget that since they took place there has risen up a generation who at that date were mere children, and who—as I have learned by several conversations on the subject—are singularly ignorant of the memorable events to which I allude. It therefore seems to me to be a duty imposed upon those who, owing to exceptional circumstances, are able to discharge it, to keep alive the knowledge of the sacrifices then made, the sufferings endured, and the brave deeds achieved by our countrymen; and, more than all, to cause our people to remember what the great King of heaven and earth has done to prepare the way for the establishment in India of that "kingdom which cannot be moved."

As our associations at Benares were gathered round General Neill, I could not but recall the only time I had ever seen him. It was at a meeting, I forget for what purpose, in the parish church of Dalry, Ayrshire. Suddenly, at the conclusion of one of the speeches, he entered the church, and appeared on the platform. "My friends," he said, slowly and thoughtfully, "I go to-morrow to join the Turkish Contingent, engaged in the Crimean war. I may never see you again. I have come here to-night to bid you farewell—to ask you not to forget me;" and then pausing for a little, he added in a quiet and solemn undertone, "and to ask you to pray for me." Before a word could be spoken out of the full hearts of his old friends he had bowed and departed.

It was this man who saved Benares and Allahabad.

The mutiny had burst forth with unmistakable fury and strength at Meerut on the 10th of May, 1857, when a general massacre of officers took place. I knew well the first who was cut down there! He had just joined his regiment. With simple truth I write it, that he was at once the handsomest young man and the most beautiful—I can use no other

PALACE INSIDE THE FORT.

Page 49.

word—I ever saw. He was a Christian, too, of the noblest mould, and altogether he was to me a very ideal in soul, spirit, and body.

It was on the 3d of June that Neill arrived a Benares after the famous scene at the Howrah station of the Calcutta Railway, which has been already described. On the same day the last telegram had been flashed from the beleaguered force in Cawnpore. Benares, as my readers can now understand, was the very center of Brahminical influence. As with most other places in India at that awful time, there were but few Europeans in it, and the native troops had things all their own way. But Neill had pushed on, and arrived just in time—for details cannot be here given—to deal such a sudden and decided blow to the mutineers as saved the city.

Eighty miles off, along the Ganges to the north, was the great fort of Allahabad. This was the king of the districts in revolt, the city of refuge for fugitives, the one rallying-place north of Calcutta. Let me try and give my readers some idea of the state of matters at this fort early in June. They may be briefly summarized: News from Meerut; indefinite rumors filling people's minds with alarms; the fort in possession of sixty invalided European artillerymen, with a wing of a treacherous native regiment and a Sikh regiment ready for royalty or plunder as it suited—Sir H. Lawrence having telegraphed not to trust them. Europeans, merchants, civilians, with wives and children, enter the fort. False news from Benares on June 5th, which cast a gloom over all. On the 6th June, no outbreak, and people more cheerful. At six o'clock in the evening of that day a parade of the 6th Native Infantry, who were in cantonments about three miles from Allahabad. These gallant and loyal men, faithful among the faithless, with great enthusiasm had volunteered to march to Delhi and to fight with us! Was it not noble of them? Their officers were justly proud; and so was government. A letter of thanks from the Governor-General was read to them on parade at six P.M., and the warm-hearted loyal men were very naturally gratified by this recognition of their services, and cheered loudly. The same evening these fine fellows broke out into mutiny, and in the mess-house of their regiment murdered in cold blood seventeen officers, eight of whom were young cadets, who, just arrived from England, were full of life and hope! Some officers escaped, and two of them, after great exertions and long swims, managed to get into the fort. But before the morning of the 7th of June thirty-one Europeans, male and female, had been massacred. "Early in the morning the jail gates were thrown open, and 3000 ruffians and many thousand miscreants from its wards, rushed eagerly to help in the deeds of that night. Soon the whole horizon looking north and west from the ramparts of the fort became one mass of flame and lurid smoke, from which issued the yells and shrieks of thousands of infuriated devils doing the work of plunder and rapine."*

The learned American missionary, Dr. Owen, described to me his feelings as, from the ramparts, he saw his house and valuable library blazing in the distance!

Such was the state of things in and around Allahabad, the Fort of Refuge, on the 6th of June. All was darkness and despair! But next day fifty (only fifty!) of Neill's regiment, the "Madras Lambs," arrived at the Benares end of the Bridge of Boats, which was in possession of the enemy. These noble fellows, "by hook or by crook," had the previous night got over the eighty miles which separated them from Benares. Yet, owing to wretched bungling, it was not till the evening that they could be got into the fort. On the 9th another detachment arrived. Best of all, on the 11th Neill himself came into view. India was then a furnace. Men fell down with sunstroke. "Fancy me," he writes, "walking a mile through burning river sand; it nearly killed me. I only lived by having water dashed over me. When I got into the open boat,

* While writing this I have before me the documents regarding the mutiny, which were furnished to the Indian government by the authorities in the districts involved in the outbreak, and which were kindly given me. The reader is referred to Mr. Kaye's forthcoming volumes as presenting the fullest and most authentic account of this memorable time.

my umbrella was my only covering. Two of our lads died with sunstroke in the boat. That I escaped is one of the greatest mercies. The Europeans cheered me when I came in. The salute of the sentries at the gate was, 'Thank you, sir, you'll save us yet.'" Neill was done up with the "terrific heat." He could not stand, but was obliged "to sit down at the batteries and give orders." But these orders were such as to clear the fort of all doubtful characters; the mutineers being beaten out of all their positions around it, the blessed telegraph could at length be flashed to Calcutta, "Allahabad is safe!"

One very touching incident is recorded in the authentic documents from which I quote, and which though narrated before may be repeated. The Moulvee or Mohammedan priest who had been at the head of the mutineers had fled, leaving behind in his terror a number of native Christians, who had been his prisoners. These were brought into the fort. "Among them was poor young Cheek, a cadet, who died the same evening, his body covered with wounds and sores, and his mind wandering. His sufferings from the night of the 6th must have been dreadful; he had escaped with severe wounds from the mess-house, and was picked up by a zemindar, by whom he was given over to the Moulvee, in whose house he had remained exposed and uncared for until this time. Nauth Nundee, a native Christian and fellow-prisoner, relates that when the Moulvee sought by threats and wiles to make him abjure Christianity, this brave young officer would call out to him, 'Never let go the faith!'"

Neill was burning to reach Cawnpore. Tremendous difficulties were in the way. And as if to deepen the already dark tragedy of woe everywhere gathering over our countrymen, there now broke out the terrible cholera. On the 18th of June it appeared in Allahabad, and, when precious gold could not be weighed against more precious men, forty out of a hundred Fusileers were cut down! But detachment after detachment was gathering at the fort. Women and children were sent down by steamers to Benares. On the 30th of June General Neill was sending off a small force of four hundred of his noble Fusileers, four hundred and fifty native cavalry, Sikhs and Irregulars, to Cawnpore. Havelock had arrived at Allahabad on July 1. By the 7th he had started for Cawnpore, and by the 15th he was followed by Neill. It was too late!

Cawnpore! How strange it seemed to hear that name bawled out as, just awakened out of sleep, we reached the city railway!

We drove through under the guidance of our good host, Mr. Lance. Nothing of any interest whatever is visible to the eye. The situation, dust excepted, is agreeable enough for a large military station, with comfortable bungalows; broad, beautiful, and smooth drives; ample means of recreation in assembly-rooms, clubs, theaters, race-courses; with all the driving to and fro, the making of calls, partaking of social entertainments, flirtations, gossip, and the et-cæteras of a civil and military society of English ladies and gentlemen. But were it not for the immortal associations of the mutiny, in which what is deepest and rarest in the British character came out, there is little in Cawnpore to arrest the attention of a traveler. Where once the desperate defense was made, he sees only a flat green or dusty plain; where the awful slaughter-house stood, he sees a flower garden of beautiful roses; the Ghat of the Massacre appears but a commonplace river-bank, with an insignificant-looking temple, washed by the kindly waters of the Ganges; and the well which includes the remains of those whose memory during this generation will sadden many an English home, looks only a nice bit of Gothic architecture.

But if with a fresh memory of that time, or with such an eloquent and exhaustive volume as that of Mr. Trevelyan, for example, one visits those never-to-be-forgotten places, then all is changed into a scene of intensest interest.

A few facts may be recorded to revive in some degree the memory of that sad but glorious past, and of the price paid there and elsewhere for our possession of British India.

Let the reader picture to himself a large open

space, perfectly flat, covered with dust, and surrounded by a parapet of earth about five feet high.

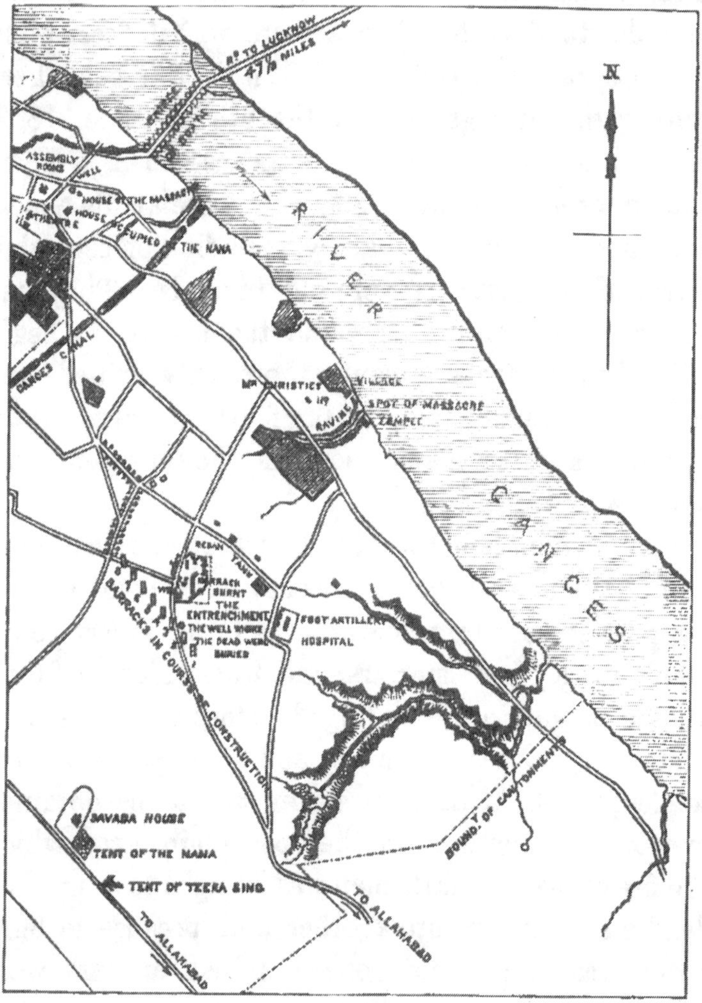

MAP OF CAWNPORE.

It was miserable shelter to those who worked guns with large embrasures! At the end of this, in the open ground, was the only accessible well. The space contained also one-storied barracks, most of them thatched. The map will enable the reader to understand better than a mere verbal description the topography of the place. Within this field there were gathered together, on the 6th of June, 1857, seven hundred and fifty Europeans—men, women, and children. Of those, fifty-nine were artillerymen, one hundred and five infantry, including officers; but thirty of the privates were old invalids. They had six guns in position. Around them were, to begin with, four native regiments thoroughly drilled, and constantly augmented, with fourteen large guns, mortars, and as many more as they needed from our deserted magazine!

Can imagination conceive this British force maintaining their position for twenty days, amid an uninterrupted roar from heavy guns firing almost point-blank range, from mortars, and from riflemen filling all the neighboring buildings? Hospital stores were destroyed; houses set on fire, and many persons burnt to death; not a drop of water was to be obtained except from one well in the open plain, upon which the fire of twenty marksmen was brought to bear. The dead were thrown into another well, because to bury them was impossible; one hundred at last were killed, and all the artillerymen among them! Yet amid hourly horrors and suffering, that handful of heroes held out in the hope of obtaining relief!

THE GHAT OF THE MASSACRE, CAWNPORE.

Page 59.

On the 26th of June the Nana offered terms of surrender. This notoriously worthless character was the adopted son of the Peishwa of Poonah, to whom, as I formerly stated, Sir John Malcolm—after the Mahrattah had played the villain and had been well thrashed for it—gave a pension of £80,000 a year, with the fine property of Bithoor near Cawnpore. His adopted son, the said Nana, inherited all the Peishwa's property, and was allowed a guard of five hundred cavalry to give him state; but he was refused the immense pension which had been granted to the Peishwa. This rankled in his breast. He was surrounded by men like-minded with himself—such men as Tantia Topee, Azim Moolah, the oily Mohammedan who, serpent-like, basked in English society, visited the Crimea, and is well described by "Russell of the *Times*," who met him there.

In utter despair, dying day by day, the garrison capitulated on being promised by the Nana a safe conduct by boat to Allahabad.

Let the reader now look at the illustration of the Ghat of the Massacre. The water is the Ganges, the building is a small Hindoo temple. Above the steep banks descending to the Ganges is a flat space of ground, and rising above it again is an inclosure, within which was a village. This spot is about a mile from the place where our people were intrenched. A narrow and rough kind of ravine for about a third of the way leads to the ghat. Down this ravine all that noble band slowly streamed on the 27th of June —sick and wounded, soldiers and officers under arms, long lines of women and children, pallid and careworn, yet thankful for any hope of deliverance. Twenty huge boats, each some twenty feet long and twelve feet broad, with thatched poops, were ranged along that bank to convey them down the stream to Allahabad. Ten thousand people from Cawnpore had gathered to see this long and grand procession, and to witness the embarkation of the wonderful people who had fought with such courage, and endured with such resolution. When they were well into the ravine, high banks rising up on either side, cavalry were drawn up across the rear, Tantia Topee and his select friends watching the whole scene from the temple. When all were entrapped and the boats crowded, the signal was given, and the thatched roofs of the boats set on fire. With the exception of three, the boats were immovably aground; and the boatmen, after setting them ablaze, leaped on shore. Then a tremendous musketry fire opened from hundreds who had till now been carefully concealed in the ground above. Guns roared from the opposite shore, from the temple, from the banks. Everywhere massacre! Struggles, blood, wounds, flame, smoke, drowning, screaming, and wild and indescribable horror of horrors! In vain two or three boats make off; in vain men swim or fight for their lives. Except two or three who escaped as by miracle, *all* the men were slain. Old Sir Hugh was cut down among the first as he was getting out of his palanquin. Wet, wounded, and bleeding, upwards of one hundred women and children were brought back to Cawnpore and locked up till wanted!

They were shortly after joined by the separate bands of fugitives from Futtyghur, about sixty miles farther up the river. A magnificent defense had been made there, also against overwhelming numbers, by about thirty men, who protected seventy or eighty women and children in a ruined fort, which they were forced to abandon. They tried by boats to reach Allahabad, but were made prisoners by the Nana's troops. All the men were butchered by him; while the women and children were added to the number already in the house at Cawnpore! There, in two rooms, twenty feet by ten, two hundred and six European ladies and children were for a fortnight pent up during the burning heat of an Eastern summer.

Havelock had started from Allahabad on the 6th July. Battle after battle had been fought until he entered Cawnpore on the 17th. But there was not a person from his suffering countrymen alive to receive him! He and his noble troops were received apparently with joy by the inhabitants of Cawnpore, who had grievously suffered at the hands of the rebellious soldiers. They gazed with wonder on the ruined intrenchments; but no English voice greeted them. Two days before, all had been massacred, and, whether alive or dead, hurled into the well, which has ever since been almost a holy place in our

MEMORIAL WELL, CAWNPORE.

memories. A beautiful garden grows its roses and other flowers where that awful slaughter-house once stood. The well has been covered by the adornments of architecture, a white marble angel of peace, by Marochetti, standing over it, and around it a protecting wall of Gothic design.

MEMORIAL WELL, WITH CHURCH IN DISTANCE.

The agents in that fearful tragedy have, I believe, gone to their account. The butchers who were personally engaged in it were all discovered and executed. I saw the spot near the ravine, where the last had been hanged. Tantia Topee, after a long chase of months, was at last run down, and hanged by Sir Hugh Rose. The Nana and his immediate followers have beyond doubt died ere now, though they were *never betrayed*—to the credit, so far, of the people. When last heard of, years ago, they were wandering in terror among the jungles and forests of Nepaul. We dare not too severely condemn our troops as blood-thirsty or cruel for the terrible vengeance which they took when any opportunity offered itself of doing so, and when all the falsehoods were believed regarding the treatment of the women and children. The sight of that bloody house and awful well fired them with a maddening passion. All natives were alike in their eyes. In each they recognized the Nana, one who had been guilty of atrocities which intensified the wickedness of the most wicked.

But in order, as far as our public influence extends, to mitigate the effects of that awful time in widening the breach already so greatly to be lamented, between us and our fellow-citizens in India, let us join in publicly confessing, with shame and sorrow, the wild and indiscriminate slaughter and execution perpetrated afterward in cooler blood, when Christian gentlemen murdered "Pandies" in a spirit which sunk them below the level of their enemies. We have not come out of the mutiny with clean hands. In many things, both before and after it, we have been grievously to blame. Many a story is doubtless told in the bazaars that would make us blush if we heard it, and make us feel that it might be fitting for us to ask forgiveness as well as to extend it. If we and the natives have endured common sufferings, we have been guilty of common sins. It should also be known to our countrymen, what was ascertained shortly after the mutiny, and has been confirmed since by the most careful investigations on the part of the India government, and often before now published,—

that there never has been substantiated any cases of mutilation, or torture, or the dishonor of any woman; that the horrors of Cawnpore were the work of the Nana only and his vile adherents; that even his soldiers refused to massacre the women and children, which was accomplished by the vilest of the vile in the city. We would remember also that while the natives cannot be expected to love the English, but naturally to dislike them as aliens in race and religion, with whom as a race there can be no real sympathy, nor bonds of anything like personal attachment, yet that *all* the most influential classes who had anything to lose generally sided with us, and very many even in the darkest hour lent us their valuable aid. We may have an underlying impression of the evil done to us, but let us not add, "by the natives," from a hasty generalization, nor darken the picture by more somber colors than those warranted by fact. And above all, let our people in India, more especially young officers, by all that is truly brave and generous, endeavor to heal this grievous wound, and so impress the natives by the force of their character as well as by the power of their arms, that the Hindoos may one day thank God for the supremacy of Great Britain.

I visited the grave-yards in Cawnpore containing "our English dead:" a new one in the Park, and an old one, large and full of tombs, in another quarter. Those burial-places in India were always to me peculiarly sad. One felt as if some wrong had been done toward every one who lay there, or that some peculiar suffering had been endured by them. Why were they not beside their own people at home? There is no grave here where a family reposes. Children are here, but their parents and brothers and sisters are far away. Young soldiers and old veterans are here, men who had just come to India full of hope and ambition, and those who, after a life of toil, were just about to leave it to spend the evening of their days elsewhere. Alone they had lived in a strange land, and alone had died. No one had been there to speak to them of the old familiar faces, nor to understand their "babbling about the green fields," in their dreams of the far-off home. Alone they were buried, with no kith or kin to follow their bier, or "fathers" to whom they could be "gathered." Alone they were left by all who knew them, to be utterly forgotten in the land of their sojourning. Every grave seems a record of long-cherished hopes never realized, and of an unexpected and premature sorrow endured by those who for years were anticipating the joy of bidding them welcome home again.

But there were some graves I visited which will not readily pass into oblivion either in India or England. Chief among these was that of the gallant Peel. With deep interest I stood beside his tomb and read the inscription—"To the memory of William Peel. His name will be dear to the British inhabitants of India, to whose succor he came in the hour of need. He was one of England's most devoted sons. With all the talents of a brave and skillful sailor, he combined the virtues of a humble, sincere Christian. This stone is erected over his remains by his military friends in India, and several of the inhabitants of Calcutta. Captain Sir William Peel, R.N., K.C.B., was born in Stanhope Street, Mayfair, on the 2d Nov. 1824, and died at Cawnpore, 27th April, 1858."

I saw another grave, which recorded the death of one whom I knew and loved. He was an officer of the 78th, and a young man of great promise. The call to arms found him in infirm health, at home with his wife and family. But full of spirit and prepared to die, he promptly responded to the summons. He fought his way with Havelock to Cawnpore, and on the day when he would have got his company and the Victoria Cross he died.

There is also a small monumental cross with this inscription, "In memory of the women and children of H. M. 32d Regiment who were slaughtered near this spot. This memorial was raised by twenty men of the same regiment who were passing through Cawnpore, Nov. 21, 1857."

But we must on to Lucknow! It is only thirty miles from Cawnpore. A railway connects the two cities. Lucknow is not, like Benares, Allahabad, and Cawnpore, on the banks of the Ganges; but is inland to the east, at right angles to the river. The

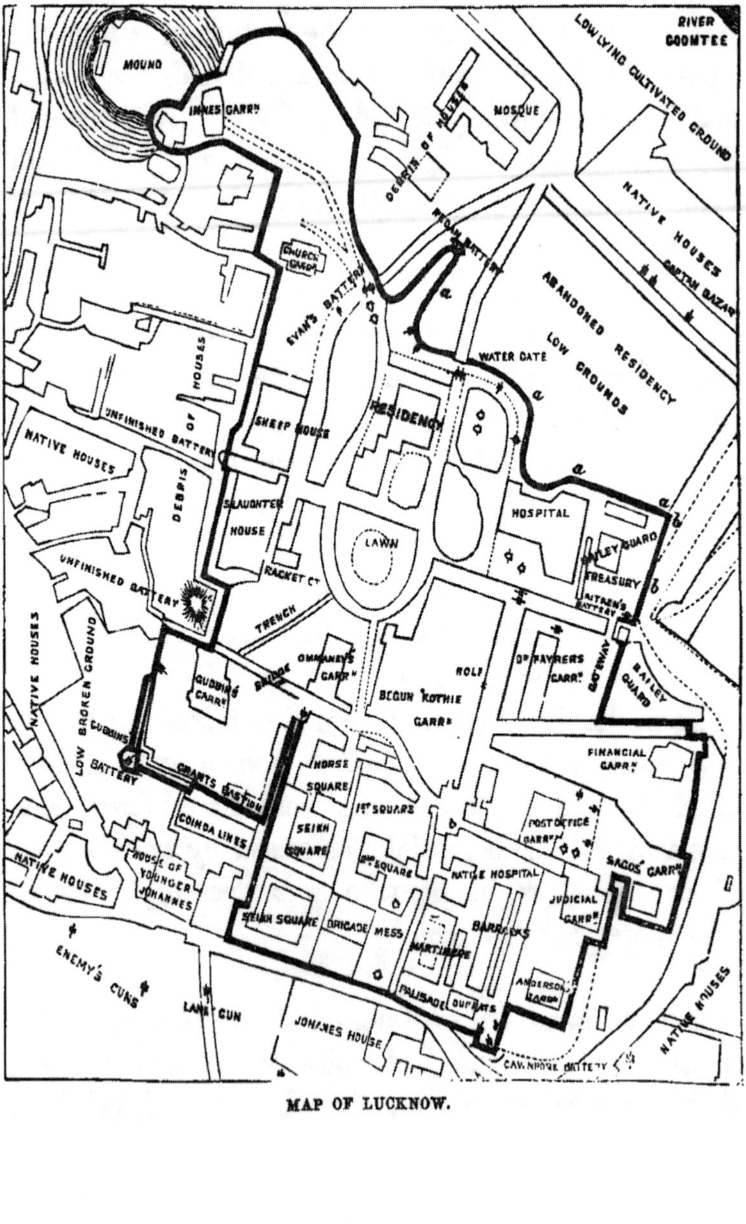

MAP OF LUCKNOW.

defense of the Residency is another Thermopylæ—for there are several in our history! It is situated on the Goomty River, about thirty miles east of Cawnpore and the Ganges. The Ganges is crossed by a long bridge of boats, and beyond is a dead flat. Among the first places seen which call up past memories, is the Alumbagh, with the small obelisk marking Havelock's grave.

We drove through the principal portions of the city; saw the spots famous in the two "advances;" paused at the arch beside which Neill was shot; ascended the roof of one of the palaces, and enjoyed a splendid bird's-eye view of the city. We noticed with deepest interest the "Martiniere," "Secunderbagh," "Mess House," and other monuments of the fierce fighting and splendid victories of the forlorn hope when delivering the long-besieged garrison. But to give the reader some idea of Lucknow, and of, to us, the most famous and interesting time in its history, let me as briefly as possible explain the illustrations which accompany this chapter.

Look first at the Kaiser Bagh, or palace of the deposed king. The view is a distant one, but it gives some idea of the imposing appearance of Lucknow. There is no other city in India so striking. It is not an Oriental city like Benares; but is rather of a European, or a sort of Parisian-Mohammedan type. From a distance it looks magnificent, notwithstanding that a great portion of it has been destroyed since the mutiny. The Residency, itself a striking object once, is now in ruins. But before the

THE RESIDENCY, LUCKNOW—EAST FRONT.

revolt the city must have stood alone in India, and even in the whole East, alike for brilliancy and beauty,—its domes, minarets, and palaces being relieved by trees and partially broken, picturesque ground, such as is rarely found in the dusty plains of Hindostan. But while its palaces looked magnificent, yet a narrower inspection revealed something flimsy about their architecture. There is a "get up," a theatrical unreality about them in spite of their wide courts, colonnades, and domes, their gilding, and orange groves, such as one sees in the Kaiser Bagh. I felt that they *did* dream "of a perishable home who thus could build." The history of the possessors and inhabitants of many of these

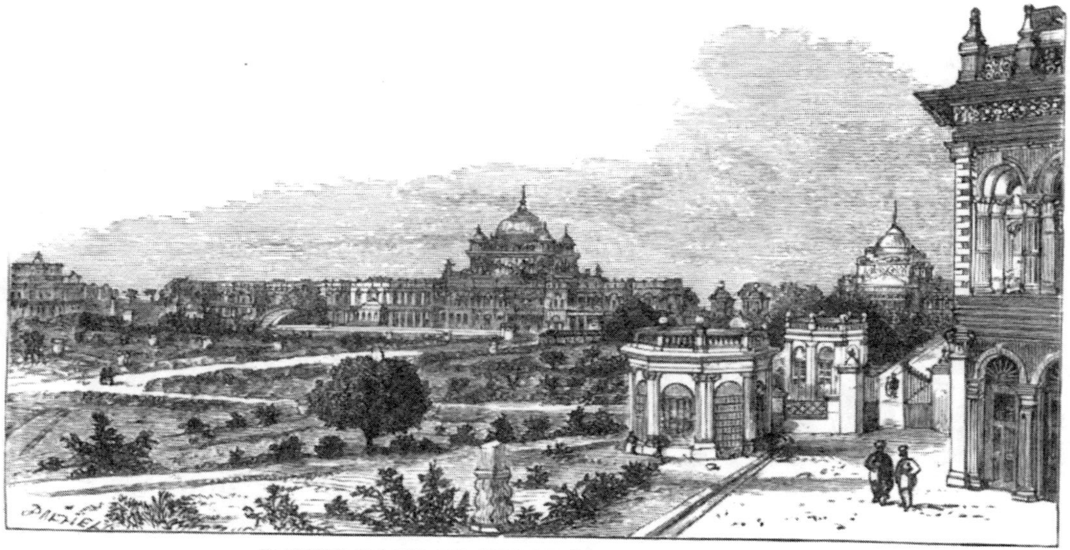

KAISER BAGH, OR KING'S PALACE, LUCKNOW.

Page 70.

splendid palaces would cause a blush to rise on the hard cheek of many a criminal at our bar. As one walked through the courts within courts of the Kaiser Bagh, there were other things of more importance than architecture to fill one's mind, and to shed a light on the history of the place. There existed not on earth a house of greater moral degradation than this! The palaces of Lucknow and Delhi were the Sodom and Gomorrah of India, and both have been utterly overthrown, never more to rise. "The king," wrote Sir William Sleeman long before the mutiny, "is surrounded exclusively by eunuchs, fiddlers, and poetasters worse than either; and the minister and his creatures worse than all. They appropriate to themselves at least one-half of the revenues of the country, and employ nothing but knaves of the very lowest kind in all the branches of the administration. The king is a crazy imbecile."

Let us now have a look at the "Residency," the home of each succeeding representative of Great Britain. It included a large portion of ground, with various buildings, such as a large banqueting-hall, guard-houses, and several official residences, grouped around the main buildings; with open spaces between, lawns, flower-gardens, etc. The Residency itself was situated on a rising ground, if a few yards above the plain can be so described.

The Europeans in Lucknow had the advantage of having in command one of the most sagacious, farsighted, and noble of men—Sir Henry Lawrence. He was fully prepared for the revolt long before it broke out, with marvelous sagacity taking in the probable future. He had kept hundreds day and night employed in throwing up such defenses as could be extemporized within a few weeks, in order that guns might be placed in the best possible position. He had also laid in such stores of every kind of provision for man and beast, as well as of every kind of shot and shell for such men and beasts as might be opposed to him, as presented a remarkable contrast to poor Cawnpore. So large was the quantity of ammunition in store that they never ran short even after having retired from the Muchee Bhowun and blowing it up with two hundred and fifty barrels of gunpowder!

A few dates and facts will suffice to enable the reader to follow our illustrations with more interest.

On May 30 the native troops revolted. There was at the cantonments the usual surprise, firings, charging, cutting down, on both sides, with splendid gallantry on the part of our officers, and all the exciting incidents of such horrible *mêlées*. After the disastrous battle of Chinhut, on 30th June, with a loss of two hundred men, our people were shut up and besieged in the Residency. There they remained till November 26th, bombarded every night by tens of thousands of native troops, who held the city and occupied the surrounding buildings,—firing eighteen-pounders within one hundred and fifty yards of the defenses; and all this during the hottest months of an Indian climate. The ladies were crowded into small rooms; huddled together in cellars to escape shot and shell; deserted by native servants, and obliged to wash and cook; to watch sick children and sick friends; to prepare meat and drink for those working in the batteries; to come into daily and almost hourly contact with disease and death and suffering in every form; to hear the incessant roar of guns and musketry; and to be prepared for the bursting of a shell or the crash of a cannon-ball at any moment in their place of retreat. What the nervous system of those thus exposed during these six months suffered, none but they who have endured the like can conceive.

After losing upwards of five hundred men on his march from Cawnpore, and fighting for four days through the streets of Lucknow, Havelock with his first relief reached the Residency on the 30th September. Food dia not increase with the numbers requiring it. But the garrison, though more straitened, was so strengthened as to be able to extend its intrenchments so as to include about two miles. The original garrison included, as Mr. Gubbins informs us, 1692 fighting men. Of these 987 were Europeans and 705 natives. There remained of the original garrison when relieved a total, including sick and wounded, of 350 Europeans and 133 natives—

23 of whom had deserted from the original number—41 military, 2 civil officers, and 1 chaplain had been killed. Early in September, before Havelock reached the Residency, there were in it 220 women, 230 children, and 120 sick and wounded.

Such facts give interest to our illustrations of the Residency. But let us look at them in detail. The first we select is "The Bailey Guard," so called, I believe, from an officer of that name who once commanded it.

The reader will notice first, the arch, or gateway of the place. Through it many a famous man has passed; among others, in those fighting days, Sir Henry Lawrence, Sir Henry Havelock, Sir James Outram, Lord Clyde, and General Neill. And through it too passed the stream of men, women, and children in solemn silence, when at midnight they left that terrible Egypt in which they had so long suffered. Every side of that arch is yet dotted by shot, marking the pitiless hail which for months had battered it from the houses now cleared away, and which once crowded the now bare and unpeopled plain.

At this arch also Outram dismounted on that joyous day in September, when the first relief and hopes of final deliverance came; and the first communications were received for a space of 113 days from the outer world of India and of Europe—when, as described by the "Staff Officer," "the garrison's long pent-up feelings of anxiety and of suspense burst

THE BAILEY GUARD, LUCKNOW.

Page 76.

forth in a succession of deafening cheers. From every pit, trench, and battery—from behind the sand-bags piled on shattered houses—from every part still held by a few gallant spirits rose cheer on cheer—cheers even rising from the hospital! Many of the wounded crawled forth to join in that glad shout of welcome to those who had so bravely come to our assistance. It was a moment never to be forgotton!"

Look again at this illustration. To the left of the arch, and beyond it, from the point of view we occupy, are seen the ruins of Dr. Fayrer's house. To this the Highlanders had pressed on, heated, worn, and dusty—for here General Outram had taken up his quarters. Mr. Gubbins, who witnessed the scene, says, "Nothing could exceed their enthusiasm. They stopped every one they met, with repeated questions and exclamations of 'Are you one of them?—God bless you!'—'We thought to have found only your bones!' At Dr. Fayrer's house a scene of thrilling interest presented itself. The ladies of the garrison, with their children had assembled, in the most intense anxiety and excitement, under the porch outside when the Highlanders approached. Rushing forward, the rough, bearded warriors shook the ladies by the hand, amid loud and repeated gratulations. They took the children up in their arms, they fondly caressed them, and passed them on from one to another to be caressed in turn; and then, when the first burst of excitement and enthusiasm was over, they mournfully turned to speak to each other of the heavy loss which they had suffered, and to inquire the names of the numerous comrades who had fallen by the way. It is quite impossible to describe the scene within the intrenchment that evening."

What a contrast to the awful silence of Cawnpore!

A very different scene had been witnessed under the veranda of that same house in July—for there Sir Henry Lawrence had expired.* Often had he been found alone in prayer during these weeks of anxiety. God's strength only could have sustained him amid weakness of body and overexertion of mind. He died (July 4) a few days after being struck with a shell which burst into his room. The last scene has been thus described:

"First of all, he asked Mr. Harris, the chaplain, to administer the Holy Communion to him. In the open veranda, exposed to a heavy fire of musketry, the solemn service was performed, many officers of the garrison tearfully communicating with their beloved chief. This done, he addressed himself to those about him. 'He bade an affectionate farewell to all,' wrote one who was present at this sad and solemn meeting, 'and of several he asked forgiveness for having at times spoken harshly, and begged

---

* His life, with that of Neill and others, was given by Mr. Kaye in *Good Words* for 1866, and is reprinted in his delightful volumes of "Lives of Indian Officers," which should be in every library.

them to kiss him. One or two were quite young boys, with whom he had occasion to find fault, in the course of duty, a few days previously. He expressed the deepest humility and repentance for his sins, and his firm trust in our blessed Saviour's atonement, and spoke most touchingly of his dear wife, whom he hoped to rejoin. At the utterance of her name his feelings quite overcame him, and he burst into an uncontrollable fit of weeping, which lasted some minutes. He again completely broke down in speaking of his daughter, to whom he sent his love and blessing. . . . Then he blessed his nephew George, who was kneeling by his bedside, and told him he had always loved him as his own son. . . . He spoke to several present about the state of their souls, urging them to pray and read their Bibles, and endeavor to prepare for death, which might come suddenly, as in his own case. To nearly each person present he addressed a few parting words of affectionate advice —words which must have sunk deeply into all hearts. There was not a dry eye there, and many seemingly hard rough men were sobbing like children.' He told his chaplain that he wished to be buried very privately, 'without any fuss,' in the same grave with any men of the garrison who might die about the same time. Then he said, speaking rather to himself than to those about him, of his epitaph,—'*Here lies Henry Lawrence, who tried to do his duty. May God* *have mercy upon him.'* And such is the simple epitaph which is inscribed upon his tomb."*

But I must ask my readers to look once more at the illustration of the "Bailey Guard"—at that portion of it to the right of the archway. "Here,"

GRAVE OF LAWRENCE.

writes Mr. Trevelyan, "from summer into winter, until of his 200 musketeers he had buried 85, and sent to hospital 76; earning his Cross in ragged flannel trousers and a jersey of dubious hue, burly Bob Aitken bore the unequal fray." I had the happiness of meeting my brave countryman, Major Aitken, at Lucknow. He told me these interesting facts: The Native Brigade, then in Lucknow, consisted of

* I had the privilege, when in Calcutta, of making Dr. Fayrer's acquintance, and of receiving from him much kindness. No man is more respected, nor occupies a more distinguished position as a medical man. I asked his friends what honors and rewards he had received from government for his services in the Residency. In this, as in too many similar cases, I received no satisfactory reply.

the 13th, 14th, and 71st Regiments. In this brigade there was only one native *officer* who joined the mutineers. In the 13th Regiment, 230 men volunteered to defend the Residency, while the remaining 750 continued faithful to us so far that they did not turn against us. *All* the native officers of the 13th Native Infantry were killed or wounded in the defense of the Residency; out of 220 men of the same regiment, 36 were *Sikhs*, of whom 18 deserted; out of 184 *Hindostanees*, 1 only deserted. Of all who defended us, 155 were either killed or wounded. During the whole time of the siege this guard-house, on to the arch, was defended by Major Aitken himself and his native soldiers *alone*, who stood firm in spite of the taunts and temptations of their countrymen, when we were in extremes. The low wall connecting the guard-house with the archway shows how slight was its defense; while the innumerable marks of shot on every spot that could be hit in the several rooms of the guard-house reveal the fierce determination both of the attack and the defense. But over that parapet wall the enemy never ventured. The well-served guns from its embrasures, and the steady rifles behind them, kept the foe at a safe distance under cover. Such facts as these ought to be recorded to the credit of the native soldiers. Many others of a like kind might be mentioned.

Let us now take another glance at the Residency, by aid of the illustration, in which the ruined banqueting-hall is the most prominent feature. During the siege that banqueting-hall, where the loud talk and mirth of the conquering race had once resounded, was the hospital of the garrison—the house of much pain, of many thoughts, and many sorrows. Here, too, Death banqueted on many a brave soldier and tender child.

Both it and the once handsome Residency, as will be seen, are now in ruins. For when the natives got possession of the place, and before it was reoccupied and restored to order by the British force, it had been all destroyed.

And now within these famous lines of defense all is swept bare with the exception of what is seen in our illustration. Great care has been taken to indicate the several famous spots—"The Cawnpore Battery," "The Redan Battery," "The site of Mr. Gubbins's House," "Dr. Fayrer's House, "Here Sir Henry Lawrence died," are all legibly inscribed on tablets, so that the stranger hardly requires a guide.

The last spot visited by the traveler will probably be the church-yard. There he will gaze in silence and with veneration on the tombs of Lawrence, Neill, and many others who "waxed valiant in fight and turned to flight the armies of the aliens," and who there lie "in the field of their fame." It is a most touching spot. The silence, with the hum of the distant city, like the murmur of a mountain-bee, contrasts strikingly with the roar of battle amid

THE BANQUETING-HALL OF THE RESIDENCY, LUCKNOW. Page 84.

which all these heroes died and had been buried. Few nations have been so privileged to record with truth the "Christian" virtues of their heroes slain in battle as we have been, on the tombs of such men as Neill, Lawrence, Peel, and Havelock. And these represent not a few of the same high character, of whom we can say—"Their very dust to us is dear!" Like the remains of Joseph, they seem to me to have already taken possession of a promised land over which the living God will yet reign.

I was struck by the memorials to some distinguished regiments, and by the absence of any memorial to others who deserved to be remembered. There are monuments erected to their comrades by the Madras Fusiliers, the 84th, the 5th Fusiliers, the 90th, and also by the Native Bengal Artillery, the 13th Bengal Native Infantry; but, strange to say, I saw none to the 78th either here or at Cawnpore!

One other scene is connected with the illustration now before us. On the summit of the rising bank which connects the plain with the slightly elevated plateau on which the Residency is built, Sir John Lawrence, as Viceroy, erected his chair of state and held a great durbar, at which the Thalookdars, or feudal chiefs of Oudh, gave in their public adherence to the British government.

It was one of those displays which arrest the senses of the spectator. Here was represented the quiet strength, the beautiful order and discipline of the various branches of our army—cavalry, infantry, and artillery—each soldier of the force suggesting thoughts of indomitable daring with which India had become acquainted, and at no place more so than at Lucknow. Here too the great lords and captains of Oudh passed slowly before the Viceroy, with six hundred magnificent elephants splendidly caparisoned, accompanied by their picturesque retainers, all glittering with gems, and arrayed in robes of many colors, made of gorgeous fabrics from the looms of Benares. It was a grand spectacle! Yet there was little in it to gratify the heart. In that wonderful procession there were some men indeed who, at considerable difficulty and risk, stood by us during our time of need, and sheltered our countrymen when, maimed and wounded, they cast themselves upon their protection. There were also not a few who had wavered and hung back, until they could discover on which side the hangman was. There were some too who never had been friendly, but had yielded themselves to our power from necessity. All, I believe, were thankful for their restored lands, and the hope of British protection to enable them to enjoy themselves while obedient. But there was not one there who loved us for our own sake;—not one who would not have preferred a native rule to ours even with *tolerable* protection of life and property; not one who did not regret the unrighteous destruction of the kingdom of Oudh, and would not have preferred its reformation, even under British coercion and protection. They gave in their submission to our government as a necessity with a smile, a shrug, or a scowl. Nothing corresponding to a British cheer could have burst from that native gathering! Nor was there any love lost on our part. The highest feeling prevalent was, I doubt not, a sincere desire to do unswerving justice to all—to protect all—curb all, and, as far as government could accomplish this, to regenerate and civilize the whole country. But that procession was seen by us—how could it be else?—through the mist of all the treachery and horrors of the mutiny. Time, however, will gradually harmonize those feelings into a mutual confidence. "Forget and forgive" will acquire ascendency on both sides. Desires for mutual considerateness, stimulated by a sense of common wrong-doing, and of common suffering, must grow in the hearts of both, and from these, again, must spring a hearty co-operation in advancing the common good of the country. Education and Christianity, under a civilized government, will yet regenerate Oudh. Our injustice to it has visited many good and true with suffering and death. Its own wickedness has annihilated its independence. But able and trustworthy natives—for there are such—will henceforth unite with able and trustworthy Europeans in administering affairs wisely and well for the good of the millions who occupy its magnificent plains.

But when the Viceroy sat in that chair of state on the green slope beneath the Residency, and beheld this recognition of British power by those who a few years before could have gained thousands of pounds by affording protection even in a stable to English gentlemen and ladies wandering in terror with their babes;—what must his thoughts have been, as he remembered that close beside him that noble brother slept "who tried to do his duty,"—how well, and how grandly, he succeeded, the spectacle before him testified.

Not undesigned was the Viceroy's choice of this spot, beneath the shadow of the Residency and of its grave-yard, for the scene we have described. There was a silent sympathy which connected the brother on his throne with the brother near him in his grave. The living said to the dead, "Thou hast not died in vain! I am here, because thou art there, and we are one in spirit, in life and in death, for I, too, like thee, will try to do my duty." England confesses with gratitude that both have done so.

CHAPTER III.

FROM LUCKNOW TO AGRA.

BELIEVING as I do that it is difficult to exaggerate the importance of the Indian mutiny—the magnitude of the sufferings patiently endured, or the deeds of heroism nobly performed;. and being convinced of the ignorance which still exists at home regarding those events which once "made the boldest hold their breath for a time,"—I shall linger for a few minutes longer amid the ruins of the Lucknow Residency, and the empty, silent courts of the Kaiser Bagh, to record a lesson or two of suffering, that may possibly deepen our sense of responsibility toward India.

I have now before me a diary kept in the Residency, by a lady, during the whole six months of the siege. Her husband and two children were shut up with her. His name, could I take the liberty of mentioning it, would recall to many of my readers those days of suffering during the disastrous retreat of our troops through the Kyber Pass, in which he bore a distinguished part. The most striking feature of this diary is its terrible sameness! Day by day, night after night, there is the same awful record of ceaseless roaring of artillery, and bursting of shells—of sudden attacks bravely resisted—of desperate sallies successfully made—of mines met by counter-mines—of deaths and midnight funerals—and of sore wounds and the sudden destruction of some beloved one by shot or shell. In reading such narratives—and how many were furnished by the year 1857 from Northern India!—we feel as if we never knew human nature before, nor comprehended how it is capable of enduring for weeks and months, slow agonies that might seem sufficient in a single night to extinguish in most people reason, if not life itself.

Here are the rapid pencil jottings of two Sundays in the same month:

Sunday No. 1.—"An attack near the European hospital during the night, but comparatively quiet here; the enemy unsuccessful. Three round shot came through the dome of drawing-room this morning. This is fearfully near, and makes us feel more and more that we know not when the day and hour of *our* call may come. May a Father in heaven have mercy on us! for his dear Son's sake make us ready! Mr. A., 7th Cavalry, shot dead, looking out from the Cawnpore battery, and Mr. H. had his leg broken from a round shot hitting a table, the leg of which broke his. Round shot of seven and nine pounds through the dome. During the night a screen made to protect from musketry at an exposed corner. Mr.

Gubbins read the service about three P.M. Mr. Polehampton, our chaplain, feared to be dying of cholera, at the European hospital, where he and Mrs. P. have been living for some time, doing much good."

Sunday No. 2.—"Poor Mrs. G.'s boy ill all night; no hope of him. Her other two children brought upstairs to be taken care of. I watched from twelve to two, and then for two hours; poor baby seemed in such pain nothing would pacify him—Mrs. B. so kind in helping me to do so; poor William, much disturbed of course; thank God, he was easy when he woke after a short sleep about daybreak; M. A. very restless and fretful. Dr. P. says it is from want of fresh air. Captain H. so good in nursing; Mrs. G. sent both my women to help him as I could not go. Messenger arrived with a letter for Mr. Gubbins, which, however, was taken *by order* at once to Brigadier Inglis, saying the relieving force was at Ounama, first march from Cawnpore, which was left in charge of a regiment intrenched, after complete victory. They had force for any opposition they might meet in coming here, and hoped to arrive in four or five days. May God prosper them! The man who brought the letter has seen the general, and said he was little, with white hair, supposed to be General Havelock. Mr Gubbins read service after breakfast; an unusually quiet day! Mrs. G. rallying; hopes of her recovery. Mr. L. killed in the Cawnpore battery this afternoon, leaving a young widow and child. They are at Mrs. ——. M. A. very feverish and heavy; baby a shade better; quite tired out, obliged to go to bed early; aroused at ten P.M. by sharp firing—an attack, but mercifully unsuccessful, and over in half an hour; but Mr. —— killed, and it is feared by our own men in cross fire. Fires in several rooms to try and purify the air."

Such were their Sundays of Rest!

Here, again, are the diaries of two successive weekdays:

"*Tuesday*, 21*st*.—About twelve, two round shot struck the house, and, from fear of others, the ladies and children moved to the dining-room—Mr. L. firing shrapnel to try and silence one of the enemy's guns which they have brought to bear on the front of the house. A European shot dead; another wounded. Good, kind Major Banks shot dead through his temples! I had just been helping their good nurse to prepare his body for *her* to see it, and had been through the sad scene with *her*, when soon after Mrs. A. told me that my own W. [her husband] was wounded. When I got to him he was lying on a couch very faint, with Dr. Fayrer examining and dressing his wound. A rifle-ball had passed through his body. God bless the doctor for his kindness. He assured me it was not dangerous. We are in God's hands. Lord, I believe, help my unbelief! I am thankful I can attend to him myself. He is in great pain. From my heart I grieve for poor Mrs. Banks!

She has lost the one that was everything to her—and their darling little girl! More barricades just outside. Some of the mutineers seem moving in bodies to-day.

"*Wednesday*, 22*d*.—A wakeful watching night! Dear W. in much pain—better, thank God, toward morning. The ladies from the other side of the house obliged to remove and go down-stairs. We were busy removing the gentlemen's things, Mrs. Dorin* assisting. When at the door leading from her room to the dining-room a matchlock-ball struck her on the face, and she immediately expired while I was looking at her and calling for a doctor! It was very awful. I had peculiar cause to think her kind and obliging, for she did much for me and mine. The enemy have moved to-day, but we know not where."

Many other extracts might be given; but I must refrain, only adding for the satisfaction of my readers, that the writer's husband and children escaped.

But there is one of many stories of suffering now before me, which I shall narrate, even although my space will not admit of my doing so in any other than the most abbreviated form.

Captain Orr, First Assistant Commissioner, commanded the native troops in Oude *before* its annexa-

---

* She was one who had escaped from the massacre at Seetapore the month before, when Mr. and Mrs. Christian, with others, were killed.

tion, and was liked by his men. He and Mrs. Orr, with their child Louisa, were at a station in Oude, about ninety miles north of Lucknow. It is called Mohumdee, and Mr. Thomason was Deputy Commissioner. The native troops rose upon the Europeans at Shahjehanpore, about twenty or thirty miles from Mohumdee, on Sunday the 31st May, while attending public worship. They massacred several, the rest escaping in various directions, and finally reaching Mohumdee. Captain Orr then intrusted his wife and child to the care of a Rajah, Lonee Singh, at Mithowlee, eighteen miles to the south, on the road to Lucknow. The escort showed Mrs. Orr and her child all respect, and made the Rajah swear to protect them before committing them to him. He sent them to a wretched, empty fort, called Kutcheanee, in the jungle. In the mean time, the fugitives from Shahjehanpore, amounting to thirteen officers, along with Captain Orr, Mr. Thomason, eight ladies, besides children, and three or four civilians, left Mohumdee for another station about twenty-one miles farther south than Mithowlee, called Seetapore. On the road the guard mutinied, and *every one was massacred!*—except Captain Orr, who was conducted by some of his old troopers to the lonely fort where his wife and child lay concealed

Two days before this massacre (June 3), the native troops had risen as suddenly as elsewhere at Seetapore, where Mr. Christian was Commissioner. Twenty-four officers and civilians were massacred, besides many women and children. The last which was seen of Mr. Christian was as he was shot dead just when he had crossed a stream, while beside his body sat his wife with a babe in her arms! They, too, were soon killed. Lieutenant Barnes, in flying for the jungle with Sergeant Morton, managed to pick up their little child, Sophie Christian, three years old. Sir Mountstuart Jackson and his sister also escaped into the jungle, and all found their way, they knew not how, to the fort where Captain and Mrs. Orr and child were hiding.

For some reason or other, the Orrs, about June 7, were separated from this party and sent alone into the jungle with a few servants. This jungle was not a forest, but an arid wilderness, with patches of thorny brushwood, sufficient to give shelter to tigers and wolves, but not to human beings. For ten days, attended by an old native servant who stood faithful to the last, they remained here, beneath the awful heat of an Indian summer sun, with no shelter but such as a few rags could afford. They were then allowed to return to the miserable fort for a few weeks, and to join their companions in misery. By this time (June 30) the Residency in Lucknow was besieged, so that no aid could reach them from its garrison.

Once more the Orrs (August 6) were separated from their fellow-prisoners and sent by themselves to the jungle, where they passed a fearful time till 20th October—suffering from jungle fever, often deluged by torrents of rain, and every day subjected to the furnace heat of a cloudless sky. The only authentic news which reached them was of the massacre at Cawnpore; and, what was more cheerful, the advance of the British troops.

Captain Orr managed to communicate with Havelock and Outram on the 20th of September, when they were about to enter Lucknow. Outram wrote to the Rajah Lonee Singh, bidding him take heed how he treated the wanderers. It had no effect. All believed the English Raj to be over, and acted as if the rebel power alone was to be conciliated. At this time an ungrateful wretch, Zahoor-ool-Hussein, who had in former days owed everything to Captain Orr, and who knew where he and the other fugitives were located, betrayed them, from self-interested motives, to the rebel government in Lucknow; and on the 20th of October a strong guard of cavalry and two guns were sent to conduct them, together with their fellow-prisoners, to the capital. The ladies were put into rude cars without any shelter. When Mrs. Orr complained and asked to be allowed to retain a sheet for the protection of the children, she was knocked down by a rude blow from a trooper. The gentlemen, emaciated by jungle fever, and suffering in body and mind, were bound with iron manacles and forced to walk. Poor Barnes lost his reason;

and Sergeant Morton fell into a convulsive fit in his agony. A cord to ease the irons by lifting them up with the hand was refused. They suffered from excruciating thirst; coarse food was flung to them like dogs once a day; and they had to march in rags, without shoes, from daybreak till sunset, with brief intervals of rest, from the 20th till the 26th of October, when, at last, amid a jeering and mocking mob, and in an agony of thirst which made the ladies scream, but scream in vain, for water, they were thrust into a vile room in the Palace of the Kaiser Bagh.

Let it be noted, that as Captain Orr marched through the streets of Lucknow he observed some of his old soldiers in the crowd weeping like children! It was these same men who had saved his life, when all others, as narrated, were massacred, on the journey to Seetapore from Mohumdee. Truly, the native character is a great riddle. The simplicity and kindness of the child, with the cunning of the fox, and the ferocity of the tiger, are most mysteriously blended.

The miserable fugitives were confined to one room in the Kaiser Bagh, under a strong guard. The sufferings of the ladies and children were unspeakable! They had been deprived, for example, of the necessary comforts of a comb or brush for months, and their hair was matted. But enough on these and other points! The garrison, in which were two of

Captain Orr's brothers, was made acquainted with their state. But no relief could be sent. From October 26 till November 16 many devices were tried by their jailers to make capital out of the prisoners at the expense of their honor; but in vain. Barnes was imbecile; Morton dying; Sir M. Jackson getting weaker every day; Captain Orr so altered as to be hardly recognized by old friends; and what of the ladies and children?

Sir Colin Campbell had arrived and taken the Residency. It was soon emptied of its defenders, who were on their way—*home!* But the prisoners still remained in the palace, while their enemies, mad with revenge, believed that the English would return no more. Strange to the captives, however, was the fact that a large force remained encamped near Lucknow at the Alum Bagh! What could this mean? There was one ray of hope, they had a true friend in a certain native, called Wajid Allee, a man of kind heart and great influence among the rebels and the occupants in the palace. He was determined to save them; but there was in Lucknow also a fierce and determined enemy of the English, a very fiend in wiles, subtlety, and persevering hate—the Moulvie Ahmed Alee Shah. He was a Mohammedan priest, born in South India, and able to speak English well. Some months before, he had preached a crusade against the "Kaffir" English in the bazaars of Fyzabad, a town in Oude, about eighty miles southeast of Lucknow. He was ordered by the British magistrate to give up his arms, together with those of his followers (seven only in number), and be silent. He refused to do either; and when attacked by a company of a native regiment, he resisted until all his followers were slain but one, while he himself, after dealing many wounds, submitted on condition of receiving a fair trial. The mutiny, in the mean time, broke out, and he escaped from prison, to become the fierce leader of that Mohammedan faction which would neither give nor receive quarter. The Moulvie, like a demon, had his eyes on the captives, and kept his spies on the alert. No sooner were Sir Colin's guns heard than these poor suffering men, Captain Orr, Sir Mountstuart Jackson, Lieutenant Barnes, and Sergeant Morton, were dragged out of their place of confinement. Nothing was told to the ladies, but they anticipated all; the bitterness of death was past. A few short words at parting; then a musketry fusillade, and they knew that all was over. They were informed weeks afterward that the wearied bodies and souls of their dear ones had then found rest. Poor little Sophie Christian died in the palace, and was interred at night in her little grave. In spite of the Moulvie, Wajid Allee, who was himself suspected and carefully watched, managed by bribes, counterspies, and much cunning, to get Louisa, Mrs. Orr's child, conveyed as a corpse through the city and the camp of the Moulvie to the

Alum Bagh, which she reached alive and well.* He also managed, with extreme tact and delicacy, to get the ladies conveyed in close dhoolies to his own house in the city. But I must quote the conclusion of this story from the deeply-interesting narrative before me, compiled at the time by Mr. Hutchinson.

"Many dangers still awaited our party while passing through streets crowded with lawless and independent soldiers, but Providence guided them, and they reached their destination in safety, followed by the guard supposed by the passers-by to be one of honor accompanying a native lady of high rank. Of course the confusion reigning in the city at the time favored the passage of the party; but again the new abode was not secure against the messengers of death hurled by the British against the doomed city, and Wajid Allee removed to yet another house in the suburbs occupied by the Sultan Mahul, and Wajid Allee's wife and children, as well as by his brother-in-law's family. Here the ladies were most kindly received, clothes provided for them, and all their wants, as much as possible, attended to. The British, already masters of the Kaiser Bagh and of the principal buildings in the city. were driving the enemy from its

* "A little child named Orr was sent in to-day by a friendly native who had concealed her in the city, where there are two or three English ladies concealed by the same man. The poor little girl was carried out through the enemy in some disguise, and delivered at the Alum Bagh port." (Dr. Russell's "Diary in India," vol. i. p. 286.)

outskirts, a portion of which was still held by the Moulvie. The monster had long suspected Wajid Allee of being friendly to the English, and his object was to seize him as he had already seized Shurfood Dowlah, the Minister under the rebel administration. Communication with the British camp, though often interrupted, was still kept up with Wajid Allee, who was plunged in the greatest anxiety regarding the safety of the ladies and of his own large family.

"The Moulvie had discovered on the 18th March the abode of Wajid Allee, who, through his own informants, had been made well aware of the designs of his enemy. The position in which the ladies now found themselves was most critical, for although the British, as we have before stated, were masters of the principal portions of the city, yet the Moulvie with a considerable force still held a position in the suburbs. On the night of the 17th or 18th March, Wajid Allee wrote to Captain Orr's brother, pointing out the extreme danger in which he was placed, and begging for assistance without delay. This letter was shown to Sir J. Outram, who communicated, we believe, on the subject with General Macgregor, then with the Goorkha troops most providentially in the neighborhood of Wajid Allee's house; but the danger was imminent, the Moulvie with his men was hourly expected, and no time was to be lost. Wajid Allee begged of Mrs. Orr to write a note, explaining the difficulties and danger by which she was surrounded, to the address of any British officer; this note he should cause to be conveyed to the nearest British post. Mrs. Orr wrote a few lines which were confided to Wajid Allee's brother-in-law. This person, however, had hardly left the house when he encountered a body of Goorkhas under the command of two British officers, Captains MacNeil and Bogle. He immediately explained to them the nature of his errand, and led the way to the house.

"The Moulvie was already from another quarter moving in the same direction. The officers rushed into the house, and without the loss of a moment placed the ladies in a palankeen; no bearers could be found, but the servants of the officers and some Goorkhas were pressed into the service, and Captain MacNeil accompanying the palankeen commenced his perilous journey, leaving Captain Bogle with the Goorkhas to escort Wajid Allee and his family. It must be remembered that Captain MacNeil had to pass through narrow streets entirely devoid of British troops, and about which the enemy were still hovering, and that he might at any moment expect an attack, or at all events a ball from some hidden assassin. Captain MacNeil, however, rushed on, urging and encouraging his party to make the most strenuous efforts. The Char Bagh ravine was reached and crossed, and in a little more General Macgregor's camp came in sight; on—on—swiftly was the palankeen borne; the friendly camp is at length gained, and the ladies are safe. It is needless to say how kindly and cordially the ladies were received by General Macgregor and his officers. Every attention was shown to them, and on the next day, the 20th March, they were escorted to General Sir J. Outram's camp, where Mrs. Orr had the inexpressible delight of once more clasping her daughter in her arms.*

"But we must return to Captain Bogle, the brave companion of Captain MacNeil. With much difficulty and at much risk he succeeded in escorting the whole of Meer Wajid Allee's family to General Macgregor's camp. The difficulty of his enterprise will be better understood by those acquainted with native manners and customs. To these officers our once captive countrywomen are indeed much indebted for the gallantry and presence of mind that they displayed on the occasion, when delay or hesitation would have been fatal. In after-years the souvenir of the deed performed by Captains MacNeil and Bogle at Lucknow will not be reckoned as the least among pleasurable reminiscences. . . . . .

"We must, however, make mention of one circumstance, the nature of which cannot but strike the most callous minds. Before the final separation of the

---

* "I went to pay my respects to two heroic countrywomen, Mrs. Orr and Miss Jackson, who had suffered so long, and so heroically. Alas! their appearance showed that they had suffered much. It was an interesting, and to me an affecting interview, and I retired sadly away." (Dr. Russell's "Indian Diary," vol. i. p. 359.)

gentlemen from the ladies in the Kaiser Bagh, Mrs. Orr had occasion to send for some native medicines. They were brought to her wrapped up in a piece of printed paper. On glancing her eyes over it, Mrs. Orr perceived that it was a portion of a leaf of a Bible, and contained the following passage of Isaiah li.: 'They shall obtain gladness and joy, and sorrow and mourning shall flee away. I, even I, am He that comforteth you: who art thou, that thou shouldest be afraid of a man that shall die, and of the son of man which shall be made as grass; and forgettest the Lord thy Maker, that hath stretched forth the heavens, and laid the foundations of the earth; and hast feared continually every day because of the fury of the oppressor, as if he were ready to destroy? and where is the fury of the oppressor? The captive exile hasteneth that he may be loosed, and that he should not die in the pit, nor that——'

(Signed) "A. ORR, *Captain.*"

Surely it was our heavenly Father who conveyed comfort in such an unexpected way as this to the broken-hearted widow from her husband! But we must bid farewell to Lucknow, which will be forever memorable in the annals of our Eastern Empire as the scene of much suffering, and of heroism never surpassed.*

---

* A most interesting volume was published by Mr. Edwards, late judge of the high court of Agra, called "Reminiscences of a Bengal Civilian." His narrative of adventure and escape during the mutiny is very characteristic of that awful time, as well as most exciting.

Agra, our next stage, opened up a new world to me. The Western Coast of India—the whole line of travel down the ghats from Poonah to Bombay, and then from the almost unmatched harbor of Bombay to the gorgeous groves of Malabar, and the picturesque Nilgherries—had left indelible impressions of the glory of vegetation and of scenery. In the west, too, at Karli, I had seen specimens of the cave temples of the old Buddhist worship. Madras and Southern India, again, had given me my only ideas of genuine Hindoo temples. There, and there only, had I seen the vast architectural piles, the pyramidal pagodas, the inner courts, the fine arcades, the ambitious and elaborate sculpture of gods and things divine; the silence and gloomy solitudes; the ruin and decay, all marking a religion of power and influence whose sun was setting. Bengal was the field in which British power, culture, and faith were seen in conflict with an old and effete civilization, docile, subtle, polite, receptive, but without the strength of truth, self-sacrifice, or self-reliance. Benares supplied the medley of splendid Eastern manufactures, of learned Pundits, of filthy ascetics, of the lowest and most degraded fetish worshipers, of holy monkeys, and of all that the Hindooism of any age, from the present day up to that of Solomon, had ever produced, tending to the highest heavens or the deepest—mud. It stands by itself—there is nothing like it in the world, just as there is nothing like Rome, or Moscow, or Jerusalem. Cawnpore and Lucknow filled my mind with nothing but associations of the mutiny, and sundry painful questions, more than once hinted at, of right and wrong, which pertain to that time, and were more or less causes of our suffering as well as of that of the natives, and were intended no doubt to be disciplinary corrections and cures of our sins, personal and political.

But once in Agra, I felt, as I have said, that a different phase of India had suddenly opened up before me. Books have given every one a certain amount of general information regarding the Mohammedan conquest of India under Baber in the fifteenth century; and we have all visions of the Great Mogul—a designation, by the way, which historians very properly reject as unwarranted by fact, but which will nevertheless remain like many a fruit of fairy tale, or of prosaic fibbing—visions of pearls, and gold, and diamonds unlimited, of power irresistible, of cruelty as great, and of whatever a young reader of the "Arabian Nights" could desire, had he only the powerful magic charm to minister to his pleasures. But I had never before seen anything—except perhaps in Cairo, and there but very partially, and I have not yet visited Spain or the Alhambra—that gave me any true idea of Mohammedan architecture. In Agra we were as in a new world, which is Oriental, but verily not Hindoo—a splendid exotic flowering in beauty and brilliancy beside the dark and ugly forms of Vishnu and Sheva. The buildings in which this architecture is

THE

; TAJ.

seen are chiefly tombs, palaces, and mosques. Were we to recognize these buildings as symbolical, we might conclude that a Mohammedan was purity itself, both in his worship and in his life, for they are pure as alabaster—simple in their forms, and destitute of every ornament except precious stones mingling with the snowy marble, just as the flowers of spring might show themselves in the recesses of the quarries of Carrara.

The famous Taj, the gem of India and of the world, the Koh-i-noor of architecture, is situated about three miles from Agra, on the west bank of the Jumna. On approaching it one sees white marble minarets rising among trees. We halt at the grand portal of a great garden, and the entrance-hall or gate so arrests us that we feel inclined to ask, with a *little* feeling of disappointment, Is *this* the Taj?—*this* being a splendid building of hard red stone—whether sandstone or granite I cannot remember—inlaid with white and black marble and various colored stones. Its arched halls are spacious. We were conducted to the upper story, and from a great open arch beheld the Taj! All sensible travelers here pause when attempting to describe this building, and protest that the attempt is folly, and betrays only an unwarranted confidence in the power of words to give any idea of such a vision in stone. I do not cherish the hope of being able to convey any true impression of the magnificence and beauty of the Taj, but nevertheless I cannot be silent about it.

From the arch in the gateway the eye follows a long, broad, marble canal, often full of crystal water, at the extreme end of which rises the platform on which the Taj is built. Each side of the white marble canal is bordered by tall, dark cypress-trees, and on feast days about eighty fountains—twenty-two being in the center—fling their cooling spray along its whole length, while trees of every shade, and plants of sweetest odor, fill the rest of the garden The buildings which make up the Taj are all erected on a platform about twenty feet high and occupying a space of about three hundred and fifty feet square. These buildings consist of the tomb itself, which is an octagon, surmounted by an egg-shaped dome of about seventy feet in circumference; and of four minarets about a hundred and fifty feet high, which shoot up like columns of light into the blue sky. One feature peculiar to itself is its perfect purity; for all portions of the Taj—the great platform, the sky-piercing minarets, the building proper—are of *pure white marble!* The only exception—but what an exception!—is the beautiful ornamented work of an exquisite flower pattern, which wreathes the doors and wanders toward the dome, one huge mosaic of inlaid stones of different colors. Imagine if you can such a building as this—

> "White as the snows of Apennine
> Indurated by frost,"

rising amid the trees of an Eastern garden rich in

THE TAJ AND GARDENS.

Page 112.

color, fruit, and flower, and standing against a sky of ethereal blue, with nothing to break its repose save the gleaming wings of flocks of paroquets adding to the glory of color; and all seen in perfect silence, with no painful associations to disturb the mind, or throw it out of harmony with the pleasing memories of a wife and mother buried here by a husband who loved her for twenty years of married life, and who lies beside her!

We walk up from the great portal along the central marble canal, ascend the platform by twenty steps, and, crossing the marble pavement, enter the Taj with a feeling of awe and reverence. Our admiration is increased as we examine the details of the wondrous interior. The light admitted by the door does not dispel but only subdues the gloom within. We stand before such a screen as we have never seen equaled. Divided into several compartments and panels, it sweeps around the marble cenotaphs that lie within it, and represent the real tombs seen in the vault beneath. It is of purest marble, so pierced and carved as to look like a high fence of exquisite lace-work, but is really far more refined and beautiful; for everywhere along those panels are wreaths of flowers composed of lapis lazuli, jasper, heliotrope, chalcedony, cornelian, etc.; so that to make one of the hundreds of these bouquets a hundred different stones are required. The Florence mosaic-work does not surpass it. And all this vision in stone was raised by a Mohammedan emperor over his dream of love,—the wife who died more than two hundred years ago, when Christian kings and emperors were sent into dark and "weeping vaults"—"the longest

MARBLE SCREEN.

weepers for their funerals!"—with no ornaments save spiders' webs. When a musical note is sounded beneath this dome, how strange are the echoes from within it! They are unearthly, like those of an

Æolian harp. The slightest note wanders heavenward, and seems to be harmonized by the voices of unseen spirits, and to be drawn out into fairy echoes and vanishing re-echoes, each more faint, more beautiful than the other, as if floating away slowly like summer winds, far, far beyond the dome, into the infinite abyss of blue!

But who—it may be asked by that trying order of readers called the lovers of knowledge—was this emperor, and who was his wife, so honored? Now, one of the difficulties we have to encounter in writing about India is the absolute want of all interest in its history prior to the time when its rulers came into contact with "*our* people." The great contests of India, which were fashioning its destiny, have less interest for us than the raids of a vulgar robber and lifter of cattle like Rob Roy, or a ticket-of-leave gentleman like Robin Hood. The succession of great emperors of the olden time in India are to most of us what the riders in a horse-race are to strangers, who see but different colors trying to make their horses pass each other.

The father of the builder of the Taj, Jehanghir, was the first ruler in India who received an ambassador from England—Sir Thomas Roe, in the reign of James I. Jehanghir married a famous beauty, Niher-ul-Nissa, the widow of Sher Afgan, who, four years previously, had been assassinated by this same Jehanghir. Her name was changed, first into Noor-

Mahal, "the light of the harem," and afterward to Noor-Jehan, "the light of the world." Jehanghir, it may be noticed, as a characteristic of the politics of the times, had *impaled* eight hundred of the race of Timour, who were "in his way" to the throne.

Shahjehan succeeded him, having murdered his own brother in order to do so. He married Arzumund Banoo, the niece of "the light of the harem"—the daughter of her brother. She was a good wife, and brought to her husband several children, among whom was Aurungzebe, who was the last ruler of the united empire of the great Akbar, his great-grandfather. After burying his wife in the Taj, Shahjehan became a miserable debauchée. He has, however, been very quiet and sober during the two hundred years he has lain beside Arzumund Banoo beneath the marble dome.

The cost of the Taj, I may add, was upwards of three millions of pounds sterling! Thousands of workmen were engaged upon it for long years. So much for the price of a sentiment. Was it too much? And how shall we balance the account between sentiment and silver?

Every one in Agra, and very many beyond it, know Dr. Murray. He is wedded to the Taj. It is the object of his genuine affection. Well for the building that he has been good enough, and tasteful enough, to make it his *spécialité;* for to him chiefly is owing the perfect repair in which it is kept. He

TOMB OF AKBAR.

Page 121.

was kind enough to have it illuminated for us at night with "Roman lights," which brought out with intense vividness the beautiful details of the interior.

Another noble tomb, at Secundra, seven miles north of Agra, is that of Akbar Shah, who is justly described as one of the greatest monarchs who ever reigned. He died in 1598. "The memory of Akbar," writes Lord Hastings, when visiting his tomb, "does not belong to a particular race or country; it is the property of mankind." He was wise and just, with a real desire to promote the permanent good of his subjects, and his laws and arrangements left little room for improvement on the part of his English successors. One of the most remarkable features of his character was his toleration of every form of religious thought. He was himself a pure theist, and seems to have been repelled from Christianity as presented to him by Portuguese missionaries, who appear to have narrated to him all their own legends and fables, thus offending his religious feeling and common sense. He was a Mohammedan, with little or nothing of Mohammed, but much of Akbar himself.

The tomb is of vast size, and is situated in a garden of upwards of forty acres. It has four large majestic portals—themselves quite palaces. It is difficult, and needless in presence of the illustration, to describe this tomb. It consists of four terraces, each narrowing above the other, except the two upper ones, which are nearly of equal extent. The court is of marble, and is open to the sky, with a marble cenotaph in the center, and a marble arcade all round with arched windows, whose panes are of carved lacelike patterns, each pane having its own peculiar figure. The whole has a most beautiful and grand effect.

Royal palaces are in India, as in many other countries, within the fort of the capital. The fort of Agra is one of imposing grandeur. It is built of red sandstone. The walls are about eighty feet high. I know few more striking architectural pictures than its "Gate of Delhi." Within are all the different kinds of buildings necessary for the palace of a great Eastern emperor. There are the audience hall, the rooms for the numerous retainers, the luxurious Zenanas; the mosques for worship; not to speak of all the space and dwellings needed for the soldiery, and for arms, small and great, and for stores of provisions for man and beast. So large is this fort, that during the mutiny upwards of five thousand fugitives found refuge within a comparatively small portion of its interior. Here the great Akbar lived for many years. His hall of audience still exists, one hundred and eighty feet long, and sixty broad, supported by graceful arches. In it his throne of state rests empty on its dais, his power having passed into the hands of another Raj, represented daily by the British soldier as he paces to and fro with his glittering bayonet. The hall is now an armory. In it are deposited the

THE FORT OF AGRA. Page 122.

BALCONY OF ZENANA, AT AGRA. Page 127.

famous sandal-wood gates of the Hindoo temple of Somnauth, brought by General Nott from Guznee in Afghanistan, to which they had been carried as trophies by Mahmoud of Guznee a thousand years before. These gates had been lost to memory, and I have heard that with whatever rejoicings they were received by the Hindoos, they were the occasion of very opposite feelings on the part of the English soldiers and officers who had to conduct them south.

But the chief objects in the fort are the buildings erected by Shahjehan, who built the Taj, and sleeps in it. These consist of the Pearl Mosque, and the apartments of the Zenana. The impression made by all these buildings is much the same as that made by the Taj. As to the Zenana buildings, picture to yourselves rooms or boudoirs, call them what you please, opening one into another, all of pure marble; here a balcony supported by delicate pillars, with projecting roofs; there exquisite balustrades in delicate lacelike open patterns with no ornament save gilding;—the views extending over the country, and embracing the Taj and the Jumna. Imagine again rivulets of water streaming from room to room along marble beds; gardens of flowers, and precious exotics —the creepers running over trellises, and shading from the heat the pathways across the marble floors, and mingling with the flying spray of fountains; and this on and on, from room to room, from balcony to balcony, from court to court. And then there are two recesses impervious to heat, whose walls are formed of innumerable small mirrors, with lamps without number, by which tiny water-falls used to be illumined from behind, as they flowed into marble fonts and thence issued in bubbling rivulets or sprang into fluttering jets of spray of delicious coolness. No palaces can be imagined more full of the joyousness and poetry of mellowed light and crystal water, and of that beauty of color and form which harmonizes naturally with the blue sky and the illumined air, the green foliage and the birds of brilliant hue. The mosques are ideal places of worship, so grand and spacious, so simple, silent, and reverential, so open to the light of day and the naked heavens, as if God were welcome at any time to enter; and so unlike the dark Hindoo temples, nay, so unlike the dark and mysterious Gothic temples of Europe. And then the tombs are also calculated to impress one with the idea of respect for the dead—as if their occupants were yet alive, and therefore worthy of being recognized in such a way as to express not only what they were but are. As far as I know Mohammedanism, all this seems quite out of harmony with its ideas and beliefs; but I presume it cannot be altogether so.

The Mootee Musjid, or Pearl Mosque, is one of the most perfect gems of art in India, and so too is the Zenana Musjid beside it. Its arches open into the marble court and garden, which are bounded on the opposite side by the Palace of the Zenana, already described. The original designer of these splendid Mohammedan palaces, mosques, and tombs which are the glory of Agra and its environs, as well as of Futtehpore Sikri, and Delhi, old and new, is said to have been one Austin de Bourdeaux. This, however, is uncertain, although there were, no doubt, many European adventurers, chiefly from Genoa and Venice, in the service of "the Great Mogul."

But there is a black side to all this white marble, —dark scenes in the shades below, balancing the brilliant scenes in the heights above. Far down beneath this marble paradise for female beauty, female *ennui*, and female misery, are various lower stories and caverned vaults. These realize in their construction, and in their revelations also, all the wild indefinite horror which fired our young imaginations in reading such stories as that of Bluebeard. Deep down are seen mysterious stairs descending into empty cells and dark caverns, and from these again descending into others still deeper down, and through tortuous passages, ending apparently in nothing, yet with more than a suspicion of a something beyond, although a built-up wall interposes. We examined these mysterious and dim retreats, and we saw enough to convince us that pleasure and pain, "lust and hate," were near neighbors in Agra as in other places. Sad evidences were apparent of beings who had, from jealousy or other causes, been conveyed to these chambers of horror and there executed in the eye of God alone. In the time of Lord (then Sir Thomas) Metcalfe, some engineer officers found their way blocked up by a wall where no wall should be. They pierced through it for about eleven feet, and then, emerging upon the other side, found the skeletons of a young man and of an old and young woman. A well was there, but no means of drawing water from it. A beautiful view could be seen from the spot, but no way of escape! I saw the place. Others who have had time more carefully to explore these underground mysteries describe a well, or pit, with ropes hung from bearers across its mouth, on which skeleton bodies of females were found. Of these and other details I cannot speak from personal knowledge, but I saw and heard quite enough to convince me that Oriental splendor might exist with horrible misery. There was enough here to illustrate the selfishness of human nature in its vilest forms, and its desires of self-gratification and cruelty. Who would compare the social blessings, the intellectual possessions, the calm security for life and property, the justice and fair dealing, the spiritual and purifying influences, of the family of an educated and sincerely Christian gentleman, husband and father, living in any of our smoky, gloomy, unartistic, commercial towns, with all that any Great Mogul ever did or could possess, amid the splendors of Agra, Delhi, or anywhere else! The emperor was miserable, not less really so that his misery was but par-

THE PEARL MOSQUE.

Page 128.

tially realized by him; while the Christian workman of a free and civilized state possesses a blessedness and peace, not the less real, though not fully realized by him, such as never dawned on the mind of an Indian king.

A strange contrast was presented during the mutiny, between the ordinary silence of those marble halls of the Zenana and Pearl Mosques, and the unwonted din of the tribes and trades, high and low, European and Oriental, which crowded into them for defense; and still more so when soldiers wounded in battle lay on those pavements, bleeding, groaning, dying, tended by ladies, who then were, and at all such times are, the very angels of mercy and hope. In that fort lie the remains of Mr. Colvin, the Lieutenant-Governor, who gave way beneath the overwhelming weight of responsibility. But I cannot allow myself to record here other illustrations of that awful period.

I was conducted over the fort by Dr. Playfair, brother of my old acquaintance, Dr. Lyon Playfair. He has devoted himself, with the enthusiasm which is in his blood, to the protection and generous explanation of the architectural glories of the fort. I dare not allege that I heard it from him, nor can I condescend at this moment on particulars, yet the *impression* remains on my mind that notwithstanding the so-called repairs of the fort, and the means adopted for the prevention of thefts, yet there has nevertheless been an uncalled-for destruction of bits of architecture which should have been preserved, if necessary, under a glass case secured by lock and key.* I cannot divest myself of the conviction, which must, I am sure, have originated from fact, that some of these local authorities do not yet fully realize the sacredness of the trust committed to them. Everything which records *mind* in the past, whether in power, taste, or opinion, should be preserved as records of *man*, be he great or small, wise or foolish. But if there is any one who will do justice to the Moslem in everything, it is the learned biographer of Mohammed, Sir William Muir, the present distinguished Governor of the Northwest Provinces.

There are many other monuments of architectural beauty near Agra on which I need not dwell. But any traveler who finds it possible to visit Futtehpore Sikri should do so by all means. It is unnecessary here to give its history. Suffice it to say, that it is within a day's drive of Agra, and was built by Akbar; that its buildings remain as perfect as when erected—its tombs being like poems in marble, its palaces of rarest

* A traveler has accused the Marquis of Hastings of having committed sacrilege among some of the magnificent marble baths by having had them removed—though they were subsequently sunk in the Ganges—to present them to George IV. But a very different and perfectly satisfactory report is given by himself in his Private Journal (vol. ii. pp. 19, 20) of this transaction. His object was to preserve them from what appeared to him to be imminent destruction, by bringing them to Calcutta, "where they might somehow be employed as ornaments for the city."

beauty, and its remains, in short, so exquisite as do not exist in any other part of the earth. To my great regret, I could not command the time to visit Futtehpore Sikri, and therefore cannot describe it, although illustrations of its glory are before me. The time is not, however, far distant when British tourists will be familiar with it. The Suez Canal and Indian railways are working out a greater revolution as regards the travel of the intelligent idle, as well as the commerce of the intelligent busy, than we can anticipate.

I am sorry I was not able to devote any time to the examination of the prisons in the Northwest Provinces, as represented by that of Agra under the surveillance of my host and old friend, Dr. Moir, the son of the well-known "Delta" of *Blackwood's Magazine.* But, from all I heard in the north, I am persuaded that the prisons of this province are models, and may favorably compare with the best in Europe. For intelligence, enthusiasm, wisdom, and perseverance in his work, I will "back up" my friend Dr. Moir against any "in the same line."

I have said nothing about missions in these northern rides; but may possibly do so yet. Meanwhile we must have a peep at Delhi—and then homewards!

CHAPTER IV.

DELHI.

It was past midnight when the carriage of the Commissioner at Delhi, Mr. M'Neile, conveyed us to his residence at "Ludlow Castle." Mr. M'Neile is the son of one widely known and respected as—I must use the old familiar name—"Hugh M'Neile, of Liverpool." And here I must take leave to express the hope that the number of English who will soon visit India, and the certainty that the Suez Canal will indefinitely increase the number, will induce enterprising persons to open *comfortable* hotels in all the great cities. The more one feels the generous hospitality shown, as in our case, by fellow-countrymen, the more one realizes the pain and awkwardness of being entertained "like a prince" by gentlemen on whom one has no claim whatever. Meals at all hours; carriages at all hours; ladies, old and young, wearying themselves to add to one's comfort; dinner-parties to meet you, etc., etc.—"It is really too bad!" as the phrase is. Yet at present this cannot be helped. I was only in two hotels in India, one at Beypore and the other at Lucknow; and wretched enough caravanserais I found them. We were therefore very thankful, in spite of the feeling that we were intruders, to find ourselves in such highly-civilized and delightful quarters as those of Mr. M'Neile.

This late capital of "the Great Mogul," once so famous and romantic in all its associations, has since the mutiny sunk down into the position of a mere provincial city. Its architectural remains are the only things of present interest. But these will become more and more interesting to European travelers.

Old Delhi—called by the natives Shahjehanabad—was built by Shahjehan in 1631. There were former cities of the same name, which were permitted to die out or were destroyed with the dynasty which erected them; and their gigantic remains lie scattered far and wide for miles and miles over the plain.

The present comparatively modern Delhi, the seat of the Mogul dynasty, is about seven miles in circumference, and contains about a hundred and fifty thousand inhabitants.

As a city it has marked features of its own. Unlike the other cities I had visited, it is walled, and that too (as we found in '57) in a most substantial manner—thanks to our own engineers. Although there are many streets as tortuous and narrow as are found in other towns, I did not see anywhere that squalor and tumble-down confusion which arrest the eye in the native quarters of Bombay or Calcutta;

while one leading thoroughfare, the Chandnee Chouk, leading direct from the Lahore Gate to the Palace, is really a fine street, ninety feet wide, about a mile long, with a row of trees, a canal along its center (covered, except in a few places), and with comfortable-looking veranda-houses and good shops on either side.

The Hindoo element is quite wanting in Delhi. A different population, too, fill the streets. Stately-looking forms from the northern plains and mountains, Afghans and Sikhs, continually arrest the eye; while the general aspect of the city is wholly suggestive of Mohammedan influence, and recalls Turkey more than Hindostan.

The two famous buildings—the Palace and the Great Mosque—are associated with Delhi, just as the Taj and Fort are associated with Agra. These buildings are both, unquestionably, worthy of the capital of the once great Mohammedan empire of the East.

Our illustration of the mosque—or Jumna Musjid, as it is called—will give a better idea of its general appearance than any description could do. It wants the unity of design and the simplicity and beauty of the Taj, but as a temple of worship it is far more imposing. The ground on which it is reared was originally a rocky eminence, which has been scarped and leveled on the summit, thus forming a grand natural platform for the building, and affording space for an open square of fourteen hundred yards. This

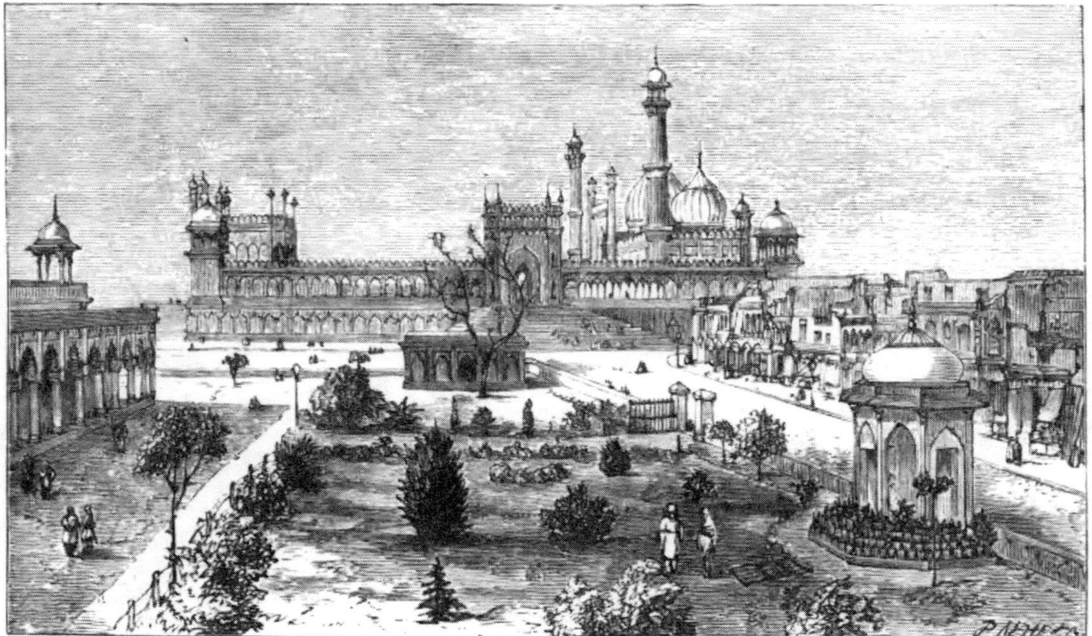

THE JUMNA MUSJID, FROM THE NORTH.

Page 138.

square has three great entrances, the most magnificent being toward Mecca. These entrances are approached by noble flights of stairs. On stepping upon the grand square, the sight is most imposing. We tread upon slabs on which tens of thousands of worshipers can kneel. On three sides are airy arched colonnades, with seated pavilions at intervals. In the center is a marble fountain for ceremonial ablutions. The mosque itself occupies the other end of the square, and is in length about two hundred and sixty-one feet. It possesses in a wonderful degree richness and beauty of color, combined with strength and grace, and simplicity and variety of form. Its general color is a deep red, from a hard red sandstone, but this is relieved by pure white marble, as in the three domes on the summit; while the minarets, one hundred and thirty feet in height, are variegated by black marble, mingling in their shafts with the red stone, and relieved by three projecting galleries of the same pure white marble as the domes. If to all this be added the marble steps leading to the mosque, and the marble roofs and walls seen within in subdued light—a cornice extending along the whole building, and divided into compartments two and a half feet broad, in which verses from the Koran are inscribed in black marble, the whole culminating in the gilt pinnacles which top the domes and gleam in the blue sky—then may the reader conceive the effect of all this—how fresh, bright, and beautiful the

Jumna Musjid is in a climate so hot, in an atmosphere so transparent, and under a sky so blue and cloudless! On entering the building, which through its giant arches seems almost an open recess from the square without, it seemed to me to be the very ideal of a place of social worship. There are no images or pictures, or anything to catch the eye or distract the attention; only the pure and unadorned marble, harmonizing with the summer sun and sky. Here thousands may meet, and do meet, for worship, without any distinction of rank, and in any dress, at any hour, and on any day; for seat-rents, and aristocratic pews for the rich only, are unknown. The Moulvie, when he has anything to say, ascends the simple pulpit, and addresses the assembled mass—his voice being audible at a great distance. The Jumna Musjid of Delhi is, in my opinion, incomparably better as a place of worship than the dark, sepulchred, bedizened, chapeled, altared, pictured, and tawdry image-crowded churches of Rome and Romanism.

We ascended one of the minarets, and had a splendid bird's-eye view of the city and its neighborhood. Immediately below is the great square; on one side, without, an open space; and beyond that again, about a quarter of a mile off, rise the huge red walls inclosing the king's palace. A number of streets radiate from the central spot which we occupied into the crowded city; while all is compactly bound by the walls and bastions embracing the city, along which the waters of the Jumna flow, on its eastern side, from north to south. Everywhere the city is relieved by green trees and the minarets of many mosques, and has a bright and cheerful look. But without the walls one catches a most impressive glimpse of that vast plain of desolation, where the cities of the past are in ruins, and their once-teeming populations lie buried, bounded only by the horizon.

There is one feature in that landscape without the walls for which I at once searched, and which, when discovered, interested me more than any other. That is the long, low, rocky ridge which rises a mile beyond the walls to the north. Questions about it were unnecessary. There is nothing else, so to speak, in the whole surrounding plain. Something seized my throat as I caught the first glimpse of this Thermopylæ where, in '57, our heroes fought, suffered, and died. But we shall have something to say of this ridge by-and-by. In the mean time let us leave the mosque and have a peep at the once-crowded home of its royal and devoted adherents.

The Palace is a great space, inclosed by red embattled walls forty to fifty feet high. The residence of a Moslem ruler must necessarily be fortified, so as to afford means of defense against any sudden *émeute* among his subjects. It must also be large enough to accommodate not only troops, but the many wives, the members of the royal family, and the innumerable officers and dependents who are connected with an Oriental court. The Palace of Delhi is three thousand feet long and eighteen hundred broad. It can afford space in its great open court for ten thousand horsemen. As to its teeming inhabitants, there were in it, when the mutiny broke out, five thousand persons, including three thousand of the blood royal!

The entrance-gate is a magnificent pile of building. A second gate admits into the great interior court, beyond which is the Royal Palace proper, consisting of the Great Hall of Audience, or the *Diwan-i-Kass*, which is two hundred and eight feet long and seventy-six broad. It is all of white marble, the roof being supported by colonnades of marble pillars. In this hall the English were first presented, two centuries and a half ago, and stood as sweet innocents before the Great Mogul—like Joseph's brethren before Pharaoh. Here the famous peacock throne once stood. It has long since disappeared, and its untold jewels have been scattered over the world since the raid and massacre of Delhi, perpetrated by Nadir Shah, in 1739. Now the Palace bears no trace of its former glory beyond these marble halls. The famous inscription remains, "If there be a paradise on earth, it is here;" but the only signs of paradise are the unsurpassed beauty and purity of the hall itself, and the absence from it of those who had made it a hell.

Most beautiful is the Private Hall of Audience; all marble, with inlaid precious stones of every hue, grouped by cunning artists; most beautiful the court

THE QUADRANGLE OF PEARL MOSQUE.

Page 128.

of the Harem, all marble also, with exquisite balconies, looking down into once-beautiful gardens on the banks of the Jumna; most beautiful too are those marble halls, where once were baths, the perfection of luxury; and not less fair that small marble mosque beside them. But, alas! the human beings who have here lived, where are they? Various travelers and writers—from the days when the Great Mogul was the admiration and envy of every nursery in which the fascinating "Arabian Nights" had charmed our Northern ancestors, down to the time of the saintly Bishop Heber—have described this place in its splendor and decay. Never did the imagination of a Carlyle even realize or picture the vision-like character of human existence which these halls suggest. We see successive crowds coming out of the inane—thundering, laughing, cursing, murdering, flashing with lightning glory over the earth; visible in beautiful women or in armed men, in the pomp and circumstance of war, in the glittering splendor of all that material earth can bestow in precious metals and more precious jewels;—we see the embodiment of irresponsible power, of unchecked self-will, mad passion, the devil, the world, and the flesh, on the peacock throne or amid its surroundings. And now, not a sound! Empty halls, vacant courts, deserted gardens; and the whole of these emperors, and shahs, and harems, and khans, and begums, with their plots, conspiracies, ambitions, and crimes, overtaken by this emptiness and awful silence! It is a terrible nightmare in history! The contrast between the present and the past, as one wanders through this palace, is oppressive!

There were many other palaces in Delhi, belonging to the native aristocracy; but these have long since been converted into public offices or residences for British officers.

Like all travelers, we, as a matter of course, visited the Kootab. We had for our cicerone the intelligent and respected Baptist missionary, Mr. Smith, who has long labored both in Oude and Delhi, and is well acquainted with the manners and feelings of the natives. Speaking of native servants, he remarked that, when kindly and justly treated, he believed them to be as honest and attached as those in other countries; and such he himself had ever found them; but he complained of the shameful treatment they often receive, especially from the military, who should know better, and an inferior order of employés. Such masters fostered the dishonesty and disobedience of which they now complain, and for which they punish their servants so unjustly and cruelly.

The drive to the Kootab is about nine or ten miles. What this Kootab is like, our illustrations of it will inform the reader as no mere words can do. One of these is of the whole of this majestic pile, giving a general idea of its appearance; the other is of a portion of its first and second stories, showing the pe-

THE KOOTAB-MINAR, WITH THE GREAT ARCH, FROM THE WEST.

Page 148.

culiarity of its structure. This tower is about one hundred and forty-three feet in circumference at its

PART OF FIRST AND SECOND STORIES OF THE KOOTAB-MINAR.

base, and is two hundred and fifty feet in height. It is built of a hard red sandstone. Four projecting galleries, at the respective altitudes of ninety, one hundred and forty, one hundred and eighty, and two hundred and three feet, divide it into four portions, each differently built from the other. The lower portion, as will be seen from our illustration, has round and angular flutings, and the second round only; while the third has only angular, and the others are smooth. A stair with three hundred and eighty steps winds within, and leads to the summit, from which a splendid view is obtained. There are also inscriptions, a foot in breadth, around the tower, containing verses from the Koran, with the names of illustrious Moslems, and the records of its builder—Kutteb-ud-din. He was originally a slave, and rose to be a general in the Turkish army. He succeeded his master, Mohammed Ghori—so called from a district of that name near Khorassan—who conquered Northern India, and became the first of the Ghori, or Pathan dynasty (1194), which was followed by that of the Moguls under Baber (1525). The Pathan capital was first here, at old Delhi, and the Kootab was a great column of victory. Around its base are most interesting ruins of a great mosque, begun by his son-in-law, Altumsh; the remains of a forest of beautifully carved pillars of Hindoo or Jain architecture, which once belonged to the palace of the conquered Hindoo Raja, being made to serve as parts of the mosque. The most remarkable of these ruins is unquestionably the series of three larger arches and three smaller ones connected with the same old building. Some idea may be formed of the central arch from the illustration. It is 22 feet wide, and 52 feet high, and covered with beautiful carving,

THE CHANDNEE CHOUK.

Page 138.

sharp as when it came from the tool. There are near the mosque two very beautiful tombs—the one of Altumsh, and the other a century later. The former is the oldest Mohammedan monument in India. Close beneath the Kootab is a remarkable pillar, consisting of a single cast of wrought iron, weighing about 17 tons, and being 50 feet in height (22 above ground) and 5 feet in circumference; the whole being without any sign of rust! This fact may interest our iron manufacturers, and puzzle them as to how such a feat was accomplished in the sixth century, about which time this pillar is supposed to have been erected. It has several very old inscriptions on it. But, as I do not attempt to turn my brief peeps into travelers' guides, I need not go beyond the illustrations in describing what I saw in old Delhi.

I could not have imagined any ruins of cities more impressive than those which cover the plains between the Kootab and Delhi. What were once streets, or the houses of the once-busy population, are now heaps of rubbish. The tombs erected to perpetuate the names of the great men of the day alone remain. But how wonderful are these!—wonderful for their size, being larger generally than the largest of our modern churches—wonderful for the elegance of their architecture, the beautiful devices of their ornaments, and the brilliancy of their colors from the combination of red stone, white marble, and encaustic tiles, all mellowed by time and made more picturesque and sad by slow and sure decay. No one takes care of them. No endeavors are made to preserve them. They are left alone in their glory. Their number, their size, their uselessness for any practical object, doom them to decay, and so they are left to time and the elements. How I wished to have had the power of the angel who carried the house of Nazareth in a single night to Loretto, that I might transport some of those gems to Scotland, and turn them into churches worth looking at!—leaving behind, however, as in duty bound, the remains of their old inhabitants in their stone boxes, and in the orthodox position with relation to Mecca.

The view given in the illustration from the roof of Humayoon's tomb on the road to Delhi is intended to convey some impression of this wilderness of ruins—so bare, stony, silent, hot!—but yet only a small portion of it, for it stretches across a space of upwards of twenty miles in its greatest breadth.

We visited, on our way to Delhi,—where I really cannot now tell,—some tombs, which have left a deep impression on my memory. Amid mounds of rubbish, along straggling paths, I recall, as in a dream, walls within walls, small courts divided by lacelike latticework, marble doors and screens, and tombs beside tombs, like some of the chapels and more splendid mausoleums in our old cathedrals—with living at-

RUINS OF OLD DELHI, FROM THE TOP OF HUMAYOON'S TOMB. Page 156.

tendants, who read the Koran, keep lamps lighted, and take *backsheesh*, and give an air of life and comfort to those abodes of the illustrious dead, which contrasted most favorably with the silent, deserted, and decaying tombs everywhere else around. In the group we visited there was, as far as I remember, the tomb of a great Mohammedan saint, Nizam-ud-din, one of the fourteenth century; and the beautiful tomb of a famous poet (Chusero), the only monument I ever heard of in India dedicated to genius only; and there was also within the same court the tomb of a princess, the daughter of the marble-building Shah-jehan, who was buried there in 1682. She is described as having been young and beautiful, and the nurse of her father during the many years of his captivity, and until he died. Her name is associated with all that is pure and noble. She desired, on her death-bed, that no canopy should cover her grave, as "grass was the best covering for the tomb of the poor in spirit." And so she sleeps with the bare earth over her, and marble splendors around her. I gazed with loving interest on her tomb. To me there is nothing more strengthening and refreshing than records of those who were good beyond their knowledge, and who walked in the light, however dim, of true love, yet knowing nothing of Him—the Light of life—from which it came. I think that princess was more than a Mohammedan saint, if what is said of her be true; and it says something for the character of the Mohammedans to have appreciated such simple goodness, and have so long believed what has been said of her as a devoted daughter and pure-minded woman. I wish such "saints" were more common and more appreciated among some professing Christians at home.

There is another tomb close by, erected to the memory of a different character, though belonging to the same noble dynasty. It is a very beautiful one, and must have cost a large sum of money. Its date is 1832. It endeavors to preserve the memory of Prince Mirza Jehangori, who died from the results of daily efforts to drink larger quantities of cherry brandy.

In passing we entered Humayoon's tomb. It is a large red building, with an immense dome of white marble, and four minarets of red stone and white marble. A great gateway leads to it through extensive gardens. Humayoon was the father of the great Akbar. Within are the cenotaphs of many of the royal scions of the Mogul dynasty, and other "superior persons." A stair leads to a terrace round the dome, and from thence the view in our illustration is taken. What gives considerable interest to this building and its surroundings is, that here Hodson secured the old king and the princes after Delhi was taken—of which more by-and-by.

The next object which attracted our attention was the old Observatory, of which an illustration is given.

THE OLD OBSERVATORY.

Page 160.

It was erected in 1728 by Rajah Jey Sing, of Jeypore, who deserves to be remembered as a man of true science, and as one who labored most earnestly and successfully in applying it practically. Five other observatories, that of Benares being one of them, were also built by him. It is unnecessary to describe all the buildings, a portion of which are illustrated. There are two equatorial dials; the size of one is, in round numbers—base, one hundred and four feet; perpendicular, fifty-six; and the hypothenuse, one hundred and eighteen.

We passed the grand old Pathan Fort, above a mile from Delhi, and beneath the archway which represents the gate of old Delhi, the capital of Feroze Shah, and destroyed by Timoor. As in the case of most ruins of towns in India, and of palaces, forts, tombs, and even tanks, not the British, but the natives themselves, were their destroyers. Delhi itself, even in the eighteenth century, was sacked by Persian, by Mahratta, and by Afghan. To intestine wars, and especially to the remorseless raids of the Mahratta powers, and to the whims and tyranny of local rulers, we are to attribute the marks of ruin everywhere visible, and the destruction of works of utility as well as beauty. Whatever decay can be charged to English neglect or parsimony has been a million-fold made up by their just administration and protection of property, not to speak of their magnificent works in irrigation, public roads, crowned by four thousand miles of railways and of telegraphic wires connecting India with the civilized world.

There are very many objects in Delhi well worth seeing and describing, but, not having had the good fortune to see them, I cannot have the pleasure of describing them, without drawing on the experiences of more leisurely tourists. Indeed, my brief notices of what I saw are merely explanatory of my illustrations. The reader may be enabled, however, by both these means to form a true idea of a few of the wonders of Delhi and its neighborhood. Those who have long resided in the country must not be offended by the attempt of a hasty tourist to describe it, nor deem me presumptuous in speaking about those glorious sights, any more than if I attempted to describe the moon and the stars as seen in an Indian sky, merely because I had gazed upon them for a few nights only, whereas "the old Indian" may have been smoking cheroots beneath them "why, sir, for thirty years! and therefore *I* ought to know something about them—but you!——"

But, after all, it is the memories and scenes of the mutiny which impress one most in Delhi. Let me endeavor, then, to aid in carrying down the story of that famous time, when our army recovered India, and at once revolutionized and saved it.*

* Those who wish to read the details of this stirring time in North India will find them admirably given in the two volumes, "The Punjaub and Delhi in 1857," written by the Rev. Cave Brown. Such volumes

Delhi was the home of a great family whose riches were gone, whose splendor had vanished, and for whose energies and ambition there was no scope. The palace was occupied by a small army of aristocratic Orientals, full of pride, but destitute of money, and subjected to every possible temptation. The idea of a mutiny was therefore a very natural one to be suggested in such a place, and, once suggested, there was much to induce the hope of its being successful. The king was an old toothless debauchee of nearly eighty, and had nothing to lose. The numer-

---

as these, and Mr. Trevelyan's "Cawnpore," with others of a similar trustworthy character, should be published in a form suited for school libraries, so that our children's children might be instructed in what their countrymen had done in "the brave days of old." Surely these are as worthy of being known as the deeds of Greek or Roman fame with which boys are crammed, and which are soon forgotten, because wanting in personal interest to them as boys and Britons. Such narratives, too, might be made truly "religious," and thus cultivate a love of country, and an admiration for deeds of heroism, endurance, and self-sacrifice. Our wrong-doing should also be confessed, that the young might learn to hate all injustice and cruelty. We can now, as we never could in former times, reproduce grand pictures of the noblest Christian faith exhibited in many a campaign in India, not by gentle women only, but by *gentle-men* and great soldiers. Our wars, when just, and our victories, are as fit subjects for religious thought and praise as were the battles of the Jews commemorated in many of the Psalms. How much more "religious" and inspiring might such volumes be made for our youth than scores which pass for this, merely because they are full of religious words and phrases and exhibit only the simpler forms of life—the strength of principle tested and revealed generally, if not always, by sickness or disease, or by a peaceful death-bed surrounded by pious and loving friends! Our young lads should be made to see how, in the camp or on the deck, in time of war and battle, men may adorn their faith in Christ.

ous princes were almost beggars, and their future was hopeless. The nobles were much in the same condition. Twenty millions of Mohammedans could be relied on as fanatical haters of Britain, and as having a traditional attachment to their king, as the representative of their race, their rule, and their faith. The whole Bengal army, splendidly drilled, with infantry, cavalry, and artillery, were with them to a man. If the handful of European troops, and of European civilians, by a bold *coup d'état*, could be cut off at once, would England cross oceans and march over plains with no captives to relieve, and attempt to reconquer India? It was a stake worth risking much for. Policy and hate, religion and race, all combined to favor the attempt. *The result showed how nearly it had succeeded!*

On the 16th of May a telegram was flashed from Delhi. It shook the nerves of the bravest in every cantonment, north and south, to which it was in a moment repeated:—"*The Sepoys have come in from Meerut, and are burning everything. Mr. Todd is dead, and, we hear, several Europeans. We must shut up!*" These words were sent by a brave man, who was immediately cut down, with his hand on the signaling apparatus. But he helped to save India and the lives of his countrymen. The mutineers were not expected so soon, even by the king. The shell had burst before its time; and but for the mysterious stupidity at Meerut on the part of those in command, the European troops there might have hindered the traitors, stained with English blood, from reaching Delhi. When clouds of dust were seen coming along the road from Meerut, caused by troopers galloping toward the city, every one wondered, except those in the secret; but these included the inhabitants of the palace and all the troops in and around the city, in cantonments and on guard; for they were, without exception, all natives. When the news spread of this sudden arrival, and when the worst suspicions were aroused, then followed the galloping hither and thither of civil servants and military officers to the guard-rooms, to the police-stations, to the palace, to the cantonments. Then there was the calling out of troops and establishing of batteries—revealing in a moment the awful fact of treachery—treachery everywhere; no one to rely on; a whole city, from the palace to the police-office, full of hate, rapidly developing into bloody thoughts and bloody deeds. The air was now filled with fierce fanatical shrieks of "Deen! Deen!" the Mohammedan battle-cry of many a revolt and massacre in the cause of "the Faith." And so it happened that ere the sun of that day set, all Europeans, with the exception of a few who had escaped like rats along the city ditch, and ladies and children who had fled to the flag-staff tower and the ridge—all were massacred, men, women, and children, by fifteen hundred mutineers, aided by all the rascally scum of that vile city. All the natives, too, who were known to be connected with us as *employés*, teachers, or students in colleges—missionaries and chaplains—native or Christian pastors, every native even speaking the English language—all were cut down in the fierce slaughter. Some who had concealed themselves were in a day or two dragged from their hiding-places, betrayed, and slain. The cantonments, too, were in arms; officers were killed; but the fugitives in the round tower managed to escape under cover of night, and then every sign of English power or sound of English speech had passed away from Delhi.

But that was not until a great deed of heroism had been performed which is fresh in the memories of most, but is unknown, I doubt not, to many at least of my younger readers. There was a small European staff over the powder magazine, consisting of some officers of artillery, Lieutenant Willoughby in command, with three conductors, one sub-conductor, and one sergeant of artillery. No assistance could be sent to them, but they would not desert their post. King's troops demanded admittance and were refused. Furious crowds of soldiers surrounded them, and began firing on the small band, climbing over the walls with ladders to seize the place. As many guns as could be mustered were crammed with grape and worked for five hours incessantly against thousands. But in vain! Most of the few defenders were wounded. Further resistance was impossible, and the last had come. But that last was terrible! Willoughby determined, if no relief appeared, to blow up the magazine, and he and his men to run the risk of being blown up with it! The train was set. It reached the foot of a fruit-tree where Scully was stationed, and it was settled that when Buckley, who was waiting for the signal from his commanding officer, should raise his hat, the fuse would be applied. Willoughby, rushing to a bastion from whence he could see the Meerut road, gave one anxious gaze—was relief coming? No! He returned to his guns; a word was passed to Buckley, who raised his hat, and the train was fired. A roar louder than the loudest thunder was heard at the flag-staff tower. The magazine, with hundreds of the natives, had been blown into the air. Poor Scully, Lieutenant-Conductor Crow, and Sergeant Edwards were killed; Tooms, Ranger, Shaw, Buckley, and Stewart, strange to say, escaped to wear the Victoria Cross. Willoughby also escaped, but he, alas! was murdered three days afterward in a village as he was making his way to Meerut. "One who saw him rush past, said that that morning had stamped years of age and care on his fair boyish face."

And now every eye was turned to Delhi, every bayonet that could be spared was pointing toward "the bloody city."

Every European soldier that could be spared from defending important military positions was mustered with all possible speed. But such troops were few; the distances were great; the heat of an Indian sun was daily increasing. The mutiny was rapidly spreading, and bursting into flames over a wide extent of country. But all that men could do would be done. Our possession of India, not to speak of the lives of all the Europeans in it, was at stake.

By the 5th of June a comparatively small force under Sir H. Barnard, marching from Umballa, was ten miles from Delhi. He was joined by another under command of Brigadier Wilson; and on the 8th of June the victory of Badlee Serai, near Delhi, was gained, and the famous ridge occupied. That ridge might seem to have been made for the purpose of keeping India under a Christian power! It never was, nor is likely to be, used for a nobler end. It rises gently from the plain, which, for a mile or a mile and a half, separates it from the walls of Delhi. Rocks like a rough comb, or dorsal vertebræ, run along portions of its summit. To the north it again slopes into a plain, where the cantonments were, and which were defended by a canal running along its whole length. It thus communicated with the Punjaub, from whence our supplies were received. This ridge is so near Delhi that the shot from its walls often passed over it, and plunged into the cantonments behind. It was flanked to the southwest by villages —like Subzee Mundee (vegetable market)—from which attacks could at any time be made under

THE CASHMERE GATE.

Page 173.

cover by the enemy. Along the summit of the ridge were some points of defense—the flag-staff house, a small mosque, an observatory, and Hindoo Rao's house.* The force which was established on the ridge did not consist of more than five thousand men of all arms. They were joined, however, next day by a few infantry and cavalry, which, beneath a burning sun, had marched from the Punjaub, five hundred and eighty miles in twenty-two days!

The enemy in Delhi was increasing daily; for to it, as the Mohammedan rallying-point, all the fine regiments of our Bengal army that were within reach—infantry, cavalry, and artillery—marched, and could not be prevented entering by our troops, as the city lay between them and the bridge of boats by which they crossed into the old fort Selimghur, now pierced by the railway. At the first the enemy were as two to one, and at the last five to one. The city was defended by a wall twenty-four feet high, with bastions, a covering glacis, ditch, etc., as seen in the illustration of the Cashmere Gate, and all in good repair, with an inexhaustible store of artillery and ammunition, used by men who had been drilled by ourselves.

* This house had been once the home of the British resident, Mr. Fraser, an excellent man, who was murdered—probably from the hatred of the people to his insolent predecessor—in 1835, by a certain Nawab and a Kuman Khan, both of whom were afterward hung for the crime near the Cashmere Gate. Hindoo Rao, who bought the house, was a Mahratta.

Cholera had accompanied our troops in the march. It never left the camp. The general in command, Sir H. Barnard, was cut down by it early in July; the previous commander-in-chief, General Anson, having died from it the day before the arrival of his successor. The next commander, General Reid, who had to retire from bad health the same month, was succeeded by Brigadier Wilson, who continued to the end of the siege. By the month of August our troops had increased to eight thousand effective men, but at the end of that month upwards of three thousand men were in hospital!

For upwards of three months we were not the besiegers, but the besieged: twenty-five attacks having been resisted. These were made by the successive bodies of mutineers who, as they arrived, were sent to prove their loyalty to the king, by trying their mettle against the British. For awhile it was all we could do to hold our own. The heat was terrific, our troops few, sickness great; and, had no assistance come, every man must have perished. Even as it was, had the cavalry in the city, amounting at one time to seven thousand men, been tolerably well handled—had there been mutual trust, instead of constant suspicion—all our supplies could have been cut off from the Punjaub, and we should have been starved out. But "God confounded their counsels." The king and his ministers were all the while, very naturally, endeavoring to rouse the great Mohammedan chiefs to rally round the banner of their liege lord, and drive the hated infidels into the sea. A reply to one of those appeals was afterward found in the palace: "Take down," it said, "the British flag from that ridge, and I will join you; but so long as it flies there, I won't!" But that flag, thank God! was never taken down until it was raised again in Delhi.

In the mean time, Sir John Lawrence, who fortunately for us ruled in the Punjaub, and was an embodiment of what the natives fear and respect—power, kindness, unswerving truth, and inexorable justice—had adopted the policy of sending every man who could be raised to Delhi, trusting for his defense against the ill-disposed to the better-disposed of the Sikh chieftains in the Punjaub. His argument was, that if Delhi fell, then all was lost, and nothing could save the Punjaub; but that if Delhi were taken, all was saved, in the Punjaub and everywhere else. He also sent men who were, each in his own way, a host in himself. Foremost was the great Nicholson, the man whom all loved and trusted, and who was literally worshiped by the natives; the man of military genius and of courage never darkened by a shade of fear; the man of such endurance that he had a few weeks before been in the saddle for twenty-four hours, pursuing the flying enemy for seventy miles without halting; the man *sans peur et sans reproche*. With him was a young engineer officer, now

Colonel Taylor, "the gallant and eminently talented," as he was described in the dispatch of General Wilson, who was fully appreciated by Lawrence, and in whom the distinguished chief in command of that arm of the service, Colonel Baird Smith, then laid aside by sickness, found a brother, who valued the true greatness, sweet temper, and perfect tact of his chief—all needed from the want of them in certain high quarters.

Nicholson, after fighting the battle of Nujufghur, and gaining a great victory, in spite of the greatest difficulties, joined the besieging army in August. The siege train arrived in September, and by the seventh of that month the first battery opened its fire. The others were soon established nearer and nearer the walls, until fifty guns and mortars poured into it shot and shell day and night from the 12th till the 14th.

On that day the final assault was delivered by several columns of attack. The one led by Nicholson scaled the breach at the Cashmere Gate, nearly at the point from which our illustration is taken. Some old Sikhs afterward, as they looked at it, knowing the tremendous odds against us, remarked to my informant, "It was not man but God who led the British soldiers across that ditch and up that wall!" The exploit at the same time of blowing open the Cashmere Gate was one of the noblest deeds in history. It was this:

The third column, under the gallant Colonel Campbell of the 52d, was to enter by this gate, which was to be blown down by powder bags. The exploding party consisted of Lieutenants Salkeld and Home, of the Engineers; Sergeants Carmichael, Burgess, and Smith, of the Bengal Sappers; and Bugler Hawthorn, of the 52d. The forlorn-hope, doomed almost to certain death, waited calmly for the signal at early dawn to advance. The firing from the batteries suddenly ceased. The bugle sounded; the rifles rushed from under cover and cheered; "out moved Home with four soldiers, each carrying a bag of powder on his head; close behind him came Salkeld, portfire in hand, with more soldiers similarly laden; while, a short distance beyond, was the storming-party, one hundred and fifty strong, under Captain Bayley, of the 52d, followed up by the main body of the column in the rear. The gateway, as in all native cities, was on the *side* of the bastion, and had an outer gateway in advance of the ditch. Home and his party were at this outer gate almost before their approach was known. It was open; but the drawbridge was so shattered that it was very difficult to cross; however, they got over it, reached the main gate, and laid their powder unharmed. So utterly paralyzed was the enemy at the audacity of the proceeding that they only fired a few straggling shots and made haste to close the wicket with every appearance of alarm. Lieutenant Home, after laying his bags, was thus able to jump into the ditch unhurt. It was now Salkeld's turn. He also advanced with four bags of powder and a lighted portfire. But the enemy had now recovered from their consternation, and had seen the weakness of the party and the object of their approach. A deadly fire was forthwith poured upon the little band from the top of the gateway, from both flanks, and from the open wicket not ten feet distant. Salkeld laid his bags, but was shot through the arm, and fell back on the bridge, handing the portfire to Sergeant Burgess, bidding him light the fuse. Burgess was instantly shot dead in the attempt. Sergeant Carmichael then advanced, took up the portfire and succeeded in the attempt, but immediately fell mortally wounded. Sergeant Smith, seeing him fall, advanced at a run, but finding that the füse was already burning, threw himself down into the ditch, where the bugler had already conveyed poor Salkeld. In another moment a terrific explosion shattered the massive gate. The bugler sounded the advance, and then with a loud cheer the storming-party was at the gateway. In a few minutes more the entire column arrived, and the Cashmere Gate and mainguard were in our hands."* But ere that day closed, sixty-six officers and eleven hundred and four men had been killed or wounded

* "Punjaub and Delhi," vol. ii. pp. 173–4. All these heroes who survived received the Victoria Cross. But, alas! after lingering several days Salkeld died of his wounds, and Home was killed soon afterward when blowing up the Fort of Malaghur.

—among them the invincible Nicholson. He had led his troop along a narrow lane between the houses and the walls to the Lahore Gate, and was mortally wounded by a shot which entered his lungs beneath his arm, as it was held aloft cheering on his men to the charge.*

Delhi was not yet won. The resistance was desperate. Its armed and now reckless thousands filled every house and house-top, and wherever room could be found to command our troops advancing through narrow streets. A third of our men under arms were disabled in the fight, which continued from the 14th to the 19th, when the city was at last wholly ours. So fierce was the struggle at one time, that the General had thoughts of withdrawing the troops. When the brave Colonel Campbell of the 52d, who had led the assault at the Cashmere Gate, heard this report, he exclaimed, "I am in, and I sha'n't go out!" To retire would have been destruction. But the troops were at first perfectly demoralized from being tempted by the wild heat and dreadful fatigue and excitement, to drink from the almost inexhaustible stores of intoxicating liquors which had been designedly laid in their way by the enemy—more deadly and dangerous than ball or bayonet. The number of bottles of

* An order arrived from the Commander-in-Chief, Sir Colin Campbell, superseding him as Brigadier-General! Red tape could do no more. Fortunately, Nicholson never heard of this. It came after his death.

spirits, etc. destroyed by order from the General is reported to have been "almost fabulous." But, nevertheless, "the wicked and rebellious city" was taken. Lucknow and Delhi, the Sodom and Gomorrah of India, had both perished. British troops bivouacked in the Great Mosque and the Palace of the Moguls, as they did in the Kaiser Bagh of Lucknow, and India was saved, to become a part of our empire from Cape Comorin to the Kyber Pass!

There was one remarkable episode of this siege, with which we conclude our sketch.

The king was never good when at his best, but now he was too old and used up in body and mind to exercise any influence or power, except by giving the authority of his name to those willing to restore the dignity of his house and to "avenge him on his adversaries." He had fled with the royal princes, and some thousands of fanatical but terrified armed followers, to take refuge, like an old toothless tiger, in the dark vaults of Humayoon's tomb, already described. Hodson heard of this. He was head of "the intelligence department" in the camp, as well as commander of "the Guides," a splendid body of Sikh Sowars. He had spies too, one at least, an old friend long known to him, in Delhi, during the whole period of the siege. He found also a willing traitor, from love of life and of *backsheesh*, in one of the king's relatives. After some diplomatic bargain-making through him with the king, Hodson was permitted to grant the worthless old man's life, and that of a favorite wife worse than himself, and of their son—if they unconditionally surrendered. After a few hours' anxious conference between the king and the "mutual friend," during which Hodson anxiously waited outside the tomb, the royal party surrendered, and straightway were conducted to Delhi, the band of followers offering no obstruction. The king entered his palace, and in the Great Hall of Audience he was received in state by the representative of Great Britain, and conveyed to prison. Ultimately, as we all know, he was transported to Rangoon and died in exile.

But his sons, the really guilty ones, were yet in Humayoon's tomb. To this Hodson next day returned. The gardens were full of an armed and infuriated mob, numbering some seven thousand, of the scum of the palace and of Delhi. Hodson had only a hundred of his "Guides." Accompanied by only one other officer, Captain Macdonald, he passed beneath the great gateway, where, as he soon learned, the princes lay concealed. With a loud voice he commanded obedience, and, entering the gardens, ordered—what sublime impudence!—the crowd to lay down their arms! He was at their mercy; for a word from any fanatic would have cut him and his companion to pieces. But they sat unmoved on their horses; Hodson smoking his cigar as a sign of calm confidence in his resources. All arms were surrendered, piled into carts, and driven to Delhi, six miles off! The princes then surrendered unconditionally, and were sent off under a guard in buggies. Hodson, with his force, then followed at some distance. Not a word had been spoken during these hours of intense anxiety; but when well clear of the tomb, and rapidly drawing with his rear-guard toward the princes, and between them and the mob, he said to his companion, "Mac! we have done it!" Yes, he had done it! done it bravely and well. It would have been well had he done no more. A man of more splendid dash and daring never charged a foe, and few possessed greater general culture and talent. But he had his failings, which it is not pleasant or necessary to allude to further. His killing of the Delhi princes is indefensible. There was neither, as was alleged, an attempt at, nor a possibility of, rescue by the rabble, whom he had disarmed. That these worthless princes deserved death is admitted, but it was for the honor and dignity of Britain that they should have been formally tried, condemned, and executed by the tribunal sitting in Delhi, as most certainly they would have been—not dragged out of their conveyances, stripped naked (to discover concealed loot?) and then shot, as was done by Hodson, with his own hand. The dead bodies were exposed for some days on an old stone platform of the mosque in the Chandnee Chouk, the spot, I was informed, occupied by Nadir Shah on the afternoon after the great massacre of Delhi.

These men and their followers deserved, no doubt, their fate. Fifteen English gentlemen and two ladies had been massacred in cold blood in the palace and city of Delhi. This was impossible without the consent, either active or implied, of those princes, who were in command. But I repeat, for the sake of the uninformed at home, what no one now denies in India, that no insults, such as we read about at the time, were offered to any of our ladies. They were suddenly cut down and slain—sufficiently terrible, no doubt—but, thank God! that was all. I feel also bound, once more, as a citizen and Christian, to acknowledge with shame our fierce and *uncalled-for* revenge, upon innocent persons too, after the mutiny; and our wholesale and cowardly executions and cruelties. I shall not prove this by giving instances, too many of which I have received from those whose names and means of information are guarantees for their truth. No good can come now from such sensational stories, but an expression of our deep regret is due to truth and righteousness. Man's nature seems to change in times of great excitement. The weak and timid often become great and brave; persons thought great and brave become sometimes athirst for blood.*

* Among other narratives which touch on those bloody deeds, the reader should consult the Diary of "Russell of the *Times*," as he is called, and Mr. Trevelyan's "Cawnpore." Since the above was in type, I accidentally met a baronet who had taken a distinguished part in the Lucknow

In thinking over these dreadful times it is a pleasing fact, that although about two thousand native Christians were involved in the mutiny, not one fought against us. Mr. Raikes, a distinguished civilian, in his "Notes on the Revolt" (p. 139), says, in corroboration of the same opinion expressed by other competent authorities, "I found it to be a general rule that when you had an official well educated at our English colleges, and conversant with the English tongue, then you had a friend on whom reliance could be placed." The mutineers, as a rule, "would trust nobody who ever knew English." He

---

campaign. On asking his opinion regarding those unworthy deeds, he said, "If a balance were drawn between the cruelties of the natives, and of our soldiers and officers in India, I fear there would be little mercy to our credit." It was very awful! "The least said, soonest mended." Let the dead bury their dead. Thank God for Lawrence, Canning, and many others who stayed the arm of the avenger, and were merciful and good; and thank God for the brighter day which has dawned on India, and promises to become brighter. The only cruel thing, by the way, which I saw done by a European toward a native, was just as the train from Delhi to Calcutta was moving slowly out of the station. A native servant, apparently in the attitude of salaaming, approached a vulgar-looking person who had been pointed out to me as a European engaged in some mercantile business in Delhi. The miscreant gave the native a severe blow on the face with his fist, which drew blood; the poor creature bent down, covering his face as if in pain, when a kick was administered, which reached his chest, and sent him off with a scream of agony! No one seemed to take the slightest notice. I shouted out, "You brute!" but the train moved off, and my voice was lost in the din. There was much of India's past history, and of the revolt of India, revealed in that brief scene. May such fellows be extirpated from the land!

also remarks that "the little body of native converts who had openly professed Christianity identified themselves with their co-religionists, and evinced their sincerity by accepting all the difficulties of our position, and throwing their lot heartily in with our own. Their cause and the Englishman's cause were one, and many of them sealed the confession of their faith with their blood." Why, one asks, are not Christians from Southern India, as well as the indomitable hill tribes, like the brave little Goorkas, made to form the strength of our native regiments?

There can be no doubt that all who had anything to lose, whether in Delhi or anywhere else, sincerely, and on purely selfish grounds, welcomed the return of our reign. All the blackguardism of the country had been let loose when our grasp was relaxed, *and the tax-gatherer had fled.* It is absurd, however, to suppose that the natives did not suffer. They were in fear of their lives, and were robbed of their property. It is equally erroneous to suppose that natives of power and influence did not aid us. Had they not done so, we could not possibly have maintained, far less regained, our position. I believe every man of character, influence, and property in India wishes us well, as being the only government with justice and power which has ever existed in India, or is at present possible. It may be true, as I have often heard in India, that "the natives hate us, and we them." But, please God, a truer union will be effected through the knowledge of a common Father and Saviour.

Before leaving Delhi, as a matter of course, I visited the famous ridge. I have seen almost all the famous battle-fields of Europe, with the exception of those in Spain. I have been at Marathon. But never did I feel that I was treading in the footsteps of nobler soldiers, or of men deserving more of the gratitude of their country and of the Christian Church, than those who fought and suffered here. With deepest interest I traced the trenches near the Observatory and Hindoo Rao's house, and *listened* to the silence and calm of nature, where once had swept for months the roar and storm of battle, as I had once listened all alone to the bee humming among the wild flowers at Hougoumont. I gazed on the ridge from my room in Ludlow Castle, itself once a spot of stern combat; I entered the Cashmere Gate,* and recalled the scene I have described, and walked along the lane where Nicholson received his death-wound. I visited, also, his grave, near the Cashmere Gate; and—

> "Oh, for words to utter
> The thoughts that arose in me!"

After the mutiny there was a revolt threatened,

---

* I was arrested on entering the gateway by a placard printed in large letters: "Blow the Drum!" What followed this inaugural announcement? "David Carson and his minstrels is coming!" So much for the contrasts of war and peace.

in 1858, of, if possible, a still more serious character, and which occasioned the deepest anxiety to the authorities. It was that of a number of our British troops. They supposed themselves to be—and justly, I think—unfairly treated when passed over from the Company's army, for which alone they enlisted, into the Queen's army, without receiving any additional bounty or a discharge. Letters were opened at the post-office by the authorities, which revealed a widespread conspiracy to unite and march to Delhi. It was a terrible revelation. Their counsels were discovered, and fortunately baffled, in good time; concessions were made, and, as no outbreak had taken place, nothing was said about it; and so the danger passed.

Delhi was my "farthest North." The hour had come to return to Calcutta, to embark for home, "by the doctor's orders." Apart from other considerations, it was to me a bitter disappointment not to have got a glimpse of the glorious Himalayas, the dream of my youth. But it could not be. I did little or nothing in my Northern journey for Christian missions, beyond addressing a few meetings and hearing something about the progress of the blessed work, which I cannot state here. My dear friend and companion, Dr. Watson, was to finish alone, in the North, what we had begun together in the South; and he was well able, in all respects, to do it, without my aid or counsel. We had quite a womanly parting-scene at the junction which separated us—he going with my old friend Mr. Gillan, one of our chaplains, to Meerut, and I alone to Calcutta. On I came for a thousand miles without a pause—a distance which but as yesterday took three months to accomplish, reaching Calcutta when "due."

So ended my days in North India.

I was welcomed at the station by my good friends, Dr. Charles, Dr. Ogilvie, William Craik, etc.

THE END.